The Wisdom of Fighters

Inspirational wisdom and advice from the greatest MMA and UFC fighters of all time on Self-Belief, Commitment, Fear, Positive Thinking, Mindset, Focus, Humility, and Community.

Neil C

advice. The content within this book has been derived from various sources. Please consult a licensed professional before attempting any techniques outlined in this book.

By reading this document, the reader agrees that under no circumstances is the author responsible for any losses, direct or indirect, that are incurred as a result of the use of the information contained within this document, including, but not limited to, errors, omissions, or inaccuracies.

Table of Contents

Introduction

To a Mixed Martial Arts (MMA) fighter, fighting is life. The MMA fighter's life is a life of extremes: suffering and sacrifice, pain and fear, loss, and hardship. Balanced against that are achievement, glory, fame, and fortune. They face some of life's darkest moments and experience some of its greatest triumphs.

It's not just fighters who experience these things; we all do at some point in our lives, but MMA fighters experience these feelings in some of the purest and most primal ways, and they do so far more regularly than most of us. As we will all have our own fights–with others, with our circumstances, and ultimately with ourselves–what better place to search for wisdom on how to face these battles than from those who have successfully made it the business of their lives?

The early champions of the UFC, Pride FC, Invicta, and other organisations were courageous pioneers. They had no idea whether MMA would take off and become a global phenomenon or whether it was just a passing fad that would soon be forgotten, and them along with it. Today's MMA champions and fans know that the sport is here to stay, but that doesn't make things any easier on them. On the contrary, with more security and stability, and the fame and money that comes with it, comes greater competition than ever.

No matter what era of MMA you look at, its champions are incredible and inspiring figures.

In this book, we're going to look at these inspiring figures through the lens of 150 of their most interesting, insightful, and inspirational quotes. These quotes will cover the topics of self-belief, commitment, fear, positive thinking, mindset, focus, humility, and community.

Every effort has been made to include quotes from the broadest possible cross-section of fighters from different weight classes, nationalities, backgrounds, and genders and verify every quote's attribution through multiple sources. Apologies in advance if your favourite fighter is missing; it's nothing personal; it's just inevitable that a sport with thousands of competitors cannot be fully covered in one book. Keep an eye out for volume two in that case!

This book is laid out with one quote per page, so that you can easily read one quote and its accompanying short essay each morning when you wake up or each night before bed. Some fighters have multiple quotes, sometimes even within the same chapter, but each passage is a unique addition to the prevailing wisdom of these fighters. Each following short essay is meant to inspire you, encourage you and possibly give you something new to think about that will help you deal with whatever challenges you may happen to be facing.

Humans, as social creatures, learn best from each other, and when it comes to facing life's toughest fights, who better to learn from than the unique fighters featured in this book?

Chapter 1:

Self-Belief

Self-belief is one of the key foundations for success and happiness, something philosophers, psychologists, educators, and coaches have known since time immemorial. Self-belief isn't something that people are just born with, and it isn't something you can just trivially choose to give yourself whenever you want.

Like anything else of value in life, genuine self-belief must be earned.

This chapter reviews some of the quotes and stories related to the self-belief of some of MMA's greatest fighters. Each quote touches on a different aspect of the value of self-belief, how to attain it, and what it means to have it.

By exploring the thoughts and experiences of people who risked everything and sacrificed much to attain the kind of self-belief that made them champions, we can find inspiration and motivation to apply their lessons to our own lives.

1: Michael "The Count" Bisping

"I've had ups and downs in my career, and if you look at it as a bookmaker, the odds of me becoming a world champion were never in my favour, but I never stopped believing in myself and never stopped trying."

Michael Bisping is an all-time great fighter, but he wasn't always seen this way. Most all-time greats have meteoric rises, where they seem to easily defeat everyone put in front of them until waltzing into their first title fight, winning it, and then holding the belt with multiple defences.

Bisping has a different kind of story: his story is that of a man whose self-belief sustained him for over a decade of coming close but falling short, who maintained this same self-belief through brutal losses and debilitating injury, until finally achieving what he, and perhaps he alone, always believed he could. He didn't steamroll his way to a championship; he had to struggle for over a decade, and only with incredible self-belief could he have continued chasing the championship for so long in the face of so much adversity.

He showed the power of sustained self-belief when he finally won the UFC middleweight (185 lbs) championship in a rematch against Luke Rockhold in 2016. That self-confidence continues to serve him well to this day. He continues to entertain and educate UFC fans as a colour commentator thanks to his knowledge and experience and his poise, wit, and charisma.

Bisping never let any doubts get in his way and was ready to seize every opportunity he got. We can all learn a lot about the power of sustained self-belief over time from Bisping.

2: Khabib "The Eagle" Nurmagomedov

"Climb the mountain so you can see the world, not so the world can see you."

This wonderful quote from the man who most would consider the greatest lightweight fighter of all time (and who is also in very serious contention for the greatest pound-for-pound *fighter* of all time), reminds us of the importance of the 'self' part of 'self-belief'. Khabib embodies as well as anyone the ideal that a person's faith in themself is *for* themself and comes *from within* themself.

The metaphor of climbing a mountain is as apt as it is poetic.

When reading and thinking about this quote, you might imagine a lone figure clambering up a steep cliff face, gripping hand holds with chilled and tired fingers and slowly pulling themselves up, step by step. Beneath the figure, on the rocky escarpment far below, are other figures, broken and fallen. Perhaps they lost their nerve. Perhaps they failed to properly prepare for the challenge, out of arrogance or laziness. Perhaps they looked back, down, behind them, for an admiring crowd to cheer them on, and in that moment, they slipped.

Khabib never made that mistake.

Khabib climbed his mountains without needing others to watch him, admire him, and cheer him on. He climbed them out of belief in himself that transcended any vanity or outside praise and regard. He climbed with a single-minded purpose and focus that nothing and nobody could break, and he will go down in MMA history with an unbroken 29-0 record that may never be matched.

3: Israel "The Last Stylebender" Adesanya

"Look, I can't dim my shine just because some people feel uncomfortable."

Israel Adesanya, "The Last Stylebender", is widely regarded as one of if not the most talented strikers in MMA today.

His nickname hints at his flashy style. Many consider him reminiscent of Anderson Silva, with a similar brutally unorthodox but effective counter-striking style that can leave opponents as frustrated as they are amazed. He even faced Anderson Silva early in his UFC career (and very late in Silva's) and defeated him by unanimous decision. His performance against the iron-chinned, iron-handed, iron-willed Kelvin Gastelum in 2019 was roundly considered the fight of the year, and perhaps one of the greatest fights of all-time.

However, Adesanya's career has not been without controversy.

Some ill-advised statements on the mic and via Instagram have caused Adesanya to come under fire from fans, media, and on one notable occasion, even the Deputy Prime Minister of New Zealand, Grant Robertson. Adesanya apologised for some of his most controversial remarks, but his style and personality remain undimmed, as exemplified in the quote featured above. Adesanya's ability to both recognise and apologise for his mistakes without compromising on his self-belief at the core of who he is shows an important kind of strength of character.

Making mistakes and atoning for them properly is human and necessary, but don't over-correct and compromise your core strengths and values. Adesanya became a champion because of his self-belief in his talents, and even in recognising mistakes, he defended his belt by refusing to "dim his shine just because some people felt uncomfortable."

4: Alexander "The Great" Volkanovski

"I'm like one of those little chihuahuas that thinks they're ten feet tall."

Australian Alexander Volkanovski has a unique and fascinating backstory to his MMA career.

Despite holding the UFC featherweight (145 lbs) belt, the first sport he got paid to play was rugby. How on earth could a 5'6 man whose natural fighting weight is in the featherweight division successfully compete in professional rugby, an open-weight sport dominated by big men? The quote featured above sums it up perfectly. Volkanovksi embodies the old adage that "it's not the size of the man in the fight, it's the size of the fight in the man".

Volkanovski's belief in himself got him a 'Man of the Match' award in his premiership-winning rugby match, but perhaps even more importantly, it enabled him to walk away from a rugby career and into an even more successful and lucrative MMA career.

Self-belief isn't only about succeeding in what you set your mind to, however the odds may look to anyone else; it's also about having the confidence to be open to new and potentially better opportunities when they arise. Alexander Volkanovski teaches us both lessons.

5: Cody "No Love" Garbrandt

"Self-belief is the greatest power we have as humans."

Cody Garbrandt's path to the championship of the lightweight division was in no way as easy as it might seem with a casual glance at his record.

Growing up in Appalachia, he seemed destined for the coal mines and even completed coal mining training. He was a natural talent at fighting, successfully wrestling in high school and getting into college via wrestling, while also having a successful 32-0 amateur boxing career. However, this talent for fighting landed him in street fights as often as sanctioned bouts and seemed more likely to derail his life than propel it.

That all changed at age 20 when he met a person he describes as his own personal hero: five-year-old Maddux Maple, who was battling leukaemia when Garbrandt's brother introduced them. The courage and determination of Maddux, inspired Garbrandt and together they made a pact: Maddux would beat cancer, and Cody would win a UFC championship. Five years later, in 2016, the pact was completed. Cody defeated Dominick Cruz to claim the UFC bantamweight (135 lbs) title and presented the belt to Maddux Maple, whose cancer was in remission after successful chemotherapy.

Cody always had the talent; what he needed was the belief that he was destined for more than prison or coal mining. He obtained this thanks to a courageous little boy who helped him put his own struggles into perspective. Where we get ours is up to us, but the most important thing is that we have it.

6: Jorge "Gamebred" Masvidal

"Nobody is taking my lunch money."

Jorge Masvidal is one of the scrappiest and most exciting fighters in the sport today, and that scrappy, never-back-down attitude is reflected in his words.

Like many fighters, he struggled to channel his talents and inclinations to his own benefit at first, often getting into street fights and ending up ineligible to compete in high school wrestling, despite his abilities, because of his grades. In the long run, Jorge's belief in himself and in the necessity of defending what's his from anyone who challenged him paid off.

Although he has not yet claimed a championship belt, he's a fan favourite with numerous 'Fight of the Night' performances, as well as one of the single most impressive performances in all of MMA. Despite facing off as an underdog against the much-heralded incoming undefeated champion of both Bellator and ONE FC, Ben Askren, Jorge Masvidal didn't back down for a millisecond. Both fighters charged the centre of the Octagon as soon as the bell rang, and Masvidal put Askren to sleep with a flying knee, ending the bout in just five seconds, the fastest knockout in UFC history and the consensus knockout of the year for 2019.

A defensive mindset is a double-edged sword that can have drawbacks until you learn to master it. Putting yourself in touch with your ability to defend yourself when necessary is a critical part of true maturity, self-belief, and ultimately success in whatever you want out of life.

Put simply: Nobody is taking Jorge Masvidal's lunch money.

7: Michael "The Count" Bisping

"People give me advice all the time, and I don't take a blind bit of notice."

Here's another cheeky quote from arguably England's greatest MMA fighter.

Of course, with a quote as funny as this, we aren't meant to take him 100% seriously or literally, but things are usually funny because they're true, and there's certainly a nugget of truth to be mined here. Bisping echoes the sentiment expressed in the saying, "There's nothing more useless than advice unasked for". He made this quote in the context of a question he was asked, which was framed to the effect of, "Everyone is saying you should…" Bisping's answer summed up just how much he cared about what 'everyone' was saying.

If you believe in yourself, you won't get distracted, discouraged, or put off by the unwanted advice of others. Asking for advice and considering it when making a big decision or undertaking a challenging task is undoubtedly a healthy and wise thing to do, but that's different from someone offering you advice you weren't looking for.

Bisping reminds us to consider both the source and the motivation of people who are always handing out advice for free. Another old chestnut in a similar vein that's worth remembering is, "You get what you pay for".

8: Tony "El Cucuy" Ferguson

"The torch needs to be held by somebody that's great. Because champions are made in the dark, baby. We don't need the lights and the spotlight. That stuff is for everybody else, man."

Tony Ferguson may go down in history as one of the most talented fighters to never win an undisputed championship belt. He may also go down as one of the most eccentric, often giving cryptic quotes that leave commentators wondering what he means.

This quote is more poetic than indecipherable, though.

The term *El Cucuy*, which means "The Bogeyman" in Spanish, is often associated with darkness. Of course, Ferguson doesn't mean his statement literally; by 'darkness', he means away from attention and fanfare. Portraying the champion as the torch bearer is a brilliant bit of symbolism. The champion is the one who brings the first light into darkness, leading others to safety or opportunity.

Ferguson has been an innovator, pushing the sport forward, and, symbolically, pushing the darkness back. That's what champions are for. Ferguson has always expressed this idea not just with his words, but with his unorthodox style that leaves opponents flummoxed with unexpected spinning back elbows and D'Arce chokes locked in from unusual positions and timing.

When Ferguson says that the lights and the spotlight are for everyone else, he expresses two valuable sentiments: firstly, the importance of self-belief that is centred inwardly, and secondly, that fandom and hero-worship is for the fans and the hero-worshippers, not for the one being worshipped.

9: Holly "The Preacher's Daughter" Holm

"Aim high and don't sell yourself short. Know that you're capable. Understand that a lot of people battle with a lot of things—depression, body image, or whatever else—so know that it's not just you. You're not alone."

Holly Holm is one of the most archetypically great fighters in combat sports.

She was a natural athlete, and, after being discovered by famous trainer Mike Winkeljohn in a cardio kickboxing class at 16, she quickly went on to have an undefeated amateur kickboxing career. She then transitioned to professional boxing and kickboxing. She will go down in history as an all-time great, holding world championship belts in three weight classes and defending them a total of 16 times. After dominating for a decade, she transitioned to MMA, and two quick wins later was promptly thrown to the proverbial wolves; namely, being thrown in front of the undefeated champion, Ronda Rousey, whose Olympic calibre judo skills had delivered her a string of almost-too-easy looking wins, primarily by submission.

The boxer-kickboxer Holly Holm was expected to have no answer for Rousey's judo, though nobody doubted her striking skills. Despite the undeniable skill of her formidable opponent, Holm fought with her typical poise, confidence and intelligence, maintained her distance perfectly, and ended Rousey's unbeaten title reign with a beautiful head kick. Holly Holm accepted the belt with grace and humility after scoring one of combat sports' all-time biggest upsets.

Holm's quote is particularly inspiring because it hints at the vulnerability she feels despite her almost unequalled career of achievements. Holm reminds us that inside every champion are the same doubts, fears, and anxieties that everyone else feels; the only difference is that champions nurture their self-belief to keep any negativity from interfering with their success and achievements.

10: Demetrious "Mighty Mouse" Johnson

"I don't allow people's outlook on me to dictate what I do in my life and how I live my life."

Demetrious Johnson, one of the greatest pound-for-pound fighters of all time, has undoubtedly earned the right to live his life the way he wants.

Johnson did not have it easy growing up, and as a natural flyweight (125 lbs), he didn't have it easy in MMA either, considering that when he got his start in the sport, the smallest weight class available in which to compete was bantamweight (135 lbs).

What Johnson gave up in size, he made up for in speed and technical skill, and was a perennial contender at that weight in the WEC and later in UFC after the merger. Once the UFC established a flyweight division, Johnson was off to the races, becoming the division's inaugural champion and defending the belt a record-breaking 12 times.

Apart from his almost superhuman speed and talent, one of the things that makes "Mighty Mouse" unique among MMA champions is his love for video games. When not in the gym, you can often find him streaming on Twitch under the username 'mightygaming'. Of course, this has drawn a few comments from those who apparently consider video gaming incompatible with being a professional fighter, but Demetrious Johnson obviously doesn't let any comments get him down. He became a record-breaking champion by believing in himself and living his life the way he knows best, and he's not going to stop now.

Genuine self-belief, a self-belief based on your actual abilities and your genuine accomplishments, makes you invulnerable to the unhelpful comments of others.

11: Fedor "The Last Emperor" Emelianenko

"A fighter, a real strong fighter, should always look dignified and calm, and I believe that any expression of aggression is an expression of weakness. A strong person will not be nervous and will not express aggression towards his opponent. He will be confident in his abilities and his training; then he will face the fight calm and balanced."

There's an expression in the MMA world: "Your favourite fighter's favourite fighter is Fedor Emelianenko".

In his career in Pride FC and many other organisations, from Affliction to Strikeforce to Bellator, Fedor Emelianenko has demolished a who's who of the heavyweight division for a decade, including many former UFC champions. He will go down in history among MMA fans as a top candidate for the title of the greatest fighter of all time.

His pre-fight demeanour–calm, cold, and obviously utterly unconcerned with his opponents (some may even detect a slight hint of pity for them)–only added to his mystique. And it was all the more notable how composed he always seemed when most of his opponents were larger and far more muscular looking than him. But when the fight started, Fedor's hand speed and accuracy were unparalleled, and his grappling proficiency was top tier.

This quote gives the key to Fedor's self-belief: he put in the hours at the gym every day. Fedor viewed any outward expression of aggression as compensation to hide or make up for an inner lack of strength. This is a coin of wisdom with two sides: if you wish to be calm and confident, put in the work to earn it, and if you're faced with an outwardly aggressive person, they may just be compensating for inner weakness.

12: "Ruthless" Robbie Lawler

"I just worry about myself. I'm just gonna be me and do me. If people appreciate it, cool. If not, I'm gonna still be me."

Robbie Lawler doesn't need to worry too much about whether people appreciate him or his MMA skills.

He won Sherdog.com and MMAFighting.com's Fight of the Year award three times in a row. In his going-on 20-year career, he has been a multiple-time champion in multiple weights and multiple organisations, including the UFC welterweight (170 lbs) championship. This quote helps explain the kind of self-belief that has made him such an enduring and exciting fighter.

The first aspect of the quote echoes some of the wisdom from quotes already featured above: focus on yourself, don't worry too much about what others think of you and don't worry too much about what others are doing. The second part is equally important. Regardless of what others think of you, only you can be you, only you are responsible for being you, and only you will have to, or get to, live with yourself.

Lawler's trademark in the cage is his courage and relentlessness. He hasn't won every fight he's been in, but he's never backed down and never faded away under pressure. He's still going to be him regardless, and for that, he can hold his head high.

13: Francis "The Predator" Ngannou

"I'm going to make my own heaven. I'm going to struggle for it. I'm going to fight to earn everything I dream about."

It would be almost impossible to make up a more inspiring story than Francis Ngannou's.

The UFC heavyweight champion was born in Cameroon and started working in a sand quarry at just ten years old to make ends meet. He idolised Mike Tyson growing up and eventually found a gym to train in boxing in his free time. However, he realised his opportunities for greatness were very limited in Cameroon, and so at the age of 26, he travelled alone to Paris, France. He arrived with no friends and no money–nothing but his dream and his self-belief. He spent some time homeless and living on the streets before getting a shot at an MMA gym called the MMA Factory, where he was allowed to train in the day and sleep on the mats at night.

After that, his life was on track.

On the surface, "The Predator" looks like a man destined to be a heavyweight champion, but his backstory shows how much more of a factor his incredible self-belief was than his incredible physique. There may be thousands, if not millions, of incredibly physically strong people who never achieve their dreams. Francis Ngannou didn't just make the most of his opportunities; he created those opportunities with his own sheer force of will and belief.

14: Khabib "The Eagle" Nurmagomedov

"Eagles don't stay in the cage."

Another brilliant and poetic quote from the unbeaten lightweight (155 lbs) gives us an idea of why Khabib has "The Eagle" as his nickname and works on many levels.

The immediate circumstances of the quote are the controversial confrontation between Khabib and members of Connor McGregor's corner immediately following their match. Khabib left the cage to confront them because of their taunts and rude remarks before and during the fight, then gave this quote as an explanation for his actions.

On a deeper level, we can imagine ourselves as a bird stuck in the cage of our circumstances. Will we be docile and loyal pets and learn to love our cage? Will we be like Aesop's poor nightingale that escaped only to find the outside world too cruel and harsh to be borne? Or will we be an eagle, outgrow our cage, and burst out of it, proud and free?

Breaking out of our cages depends upon how we see ourselves. If you want to escape the circumstances of your life, first, you must believe that you are like an eagle that will grow too strong to be contained by any cage.

15. Anderson "The Spider" Silva

"I'm not the best. I just believe I can do things other people think are impossible."

Some people may not agree with the first part of this quote, considering Anderson Silva will go down in history as one of the greatest fighters of all time, but certainly, nobody can deny that Anderson Silva did indeed do things other people think are impossible.

This quote speaks to what made Silva so great: he knocked out opponents with techniques that many people considered ineffective or unrealistic before he demonstrated their viability, like the reverse standing upwards back-elbow he used to knock out Tony Fryklund or the Karate-Kid-esque front kick he used to knock out the seemingly unstoppable Vitor Belfort.

This is another arrow in the quiver of self-belief: when you believe in yourself enough to discard the negative beliefs of naysayers and try things out for yourself, you can do the unexpected. Refusing to allow yourself and your potential to be limited by the pessimism of others is almost like a kind of superpower.

Anderson Silva is one of the champions that proves that what seems impossible for others is oftentimes nothing more than a secret weapon waiting to be discovered by the first person with the self-belief to try.

16. Chael Sonnen

"I'm okay with being booed."

Chael Sonnen is one of the great fighters in MMA history but what people will probably remember most about his career are his incredible charisma and trash-talking prowess.

In the Octagon and ring, Chael was a powerful and stifling wrestler, known for putting constant pressure on his opponents and grinding them down. It was an effective style that made Chael a champion in the WEC and got him many great wins in the UFC, but without his skill on the mic, Chael would probably not have the fame and notoriety that he does.

This quote shows how Chael made himself a superstar without the same kinds of winning streaks and unstoppable auras of the most dominant champions. Every fighter knows that the business side of fighting is entertainment, and the name of the game is getting fans to watch you if you want to get paid, but very few fighters can separate the fighting and business sides of MMA as Chael could. He was okay with being booed, with playing the villain, with saying outrageous things and accepting whatever came afterwards, and as a result, he was able to get millions of people to pay to watch him fight even though his fighting style was not the most exciting, nor was his skillset the most dominant.

That's another benefit of the power of self-belief: When you don't care whether strangers love or hate you, you can instead focus on doing what's best for yourself and the people who you care about most.

17: Khamzat "Borz" Chimaev

"Smash somebody. Take money."

The frank simplicity of this quote is fitting for Khamzat Chimaev.

A Chechen-born wrestler, "Borz" (which means 'wolf' in his native tongue), was able to parlay his wrestling prowess into an immigration visa to Sweden, where Chimaev now trains and lives along with his family.

This quote stands in stark contrast to more flowery and poetic metaphors about fighting but is no less poignant in its truth. It reminds us that sometimes life is simpler than we think.

Khamzat Chimaev was born in a war-torn, poverty-stricken homeland with few prospects for a comfortable life or the kind of money that could buy it, but he had the self-belief to develop the talents that he was given and create opportunities with them.

So, Khamzat set about doing what he could do to improve his and his family's situation: he started smashing people and taking money. Now he's an exciting prospect in the UFC welterweight (170 lbs) division, putting together a streak of Fight of the Night wins that should soon garner him a title shot.

18. Rickson Gracie

"A brave man, a real fighter is not measured by how many times he falls, but how many times he stands up."

Rickson Gracie is a legend of the sport in more ways than one.

In his prime, he was unofficially acknowledged as the Gracie family's greatest fighter. He would be sent out to meet the family's greatest challengers in the era before MMA became a formalised, global sport.

It was his brother, Royce Gracie, who was sent to win the first UFC events, however, as the intention was to show a smaller, less physically imposing man using their skills to defeat the biggest and most intimidating fighters they could find. Rickson himself did take on some formal matches, at first in Brazil and then in Japan, and retired with a perfect 11-0 record.

Where is he coming from with this quote, then, if he's never 'fallen'?

The truth is that as a child of Helio Gracie, Rickson was awarded his blackbelt at just 18 years of age and must have 'fallen' hundreds if not thousands of times in training. That would have taught him early on the lesson of this quote. Now, he passes that lesson on to his brothers and half-brothers in the Gracie family, to his own children, and to millions of Gracie Jiu-Jitsu students and fans around the world, all of whom will fall many times in their lives.

When you believe in yourself, you do not fear falling; in fact, you look forward to it because it only gives you the chance to stand up, stronger and wiser than before.

19. Valentina "Bullet" Shevchenko

"I know my strengths. I know what I'm good at."

With her resume, Valentina Shevchenko could be referring to any number of things in that quote.

Not only is she a champion in Muay Thai and kickboxing, and MMA, she's also fluent in three languages and has an undergraduate degree in film directing. Underneath a list of accomplishments like that is an iron-clad self-belief. Valentina Shevchenko knows the value of knowing your strengths.

One unique example of this is the interesting story of her brief foray into boxing.

"Bullet" has just two professional boxing matches to her credit, both in Peru. She defeated first Halanna Dos Santos, then Nerys Rincon, both celebrated veterans. What made her victories unique was that she 'boxed' them from her kickboxing stance and utilised Muay Thai clinch techniques to shut down their superior boxing skills and win first a unanimous decision, then a fourth-round TKO, respectively.

Her ability to ignore storms of scepticism and criticism from the boxing world and stick to her own strengths to defeat experienced veterans of another sport shows the power of self-belief.

20. Henry "The Messenger" Cejudo

"If you have a dream, don't let anyone talk you out of it."

Henry Cejudo lives up to his nickname, sharing an inspiring message with this quote.

Cejudo's own career is certainly the stuff of dreams. He won gold in wrestling in the 2008 Beijing Olympics at just 21, won a state boxing championship in Arizona in 2010, then transitioned to MMA in 2013, where he promptly went 10-0 to put himself into title contention. Although he dropped his first match to the incomparable "Mighty Mouse" Demetrious Johnson, he came back to become the first and only man ever to defeat Johnson at flyweight (125 lbs).

With this message, Cejudo reminds us to protect our dreams and our self-belief from those who would sabotage them by being aware of and critical of the motives of such nay-sayers.

Sometimes you get good advice that takes your own best interests to heart, but sometimes advice is given in order to protect the ego of its giver. Beware of those who tell you to give up on your dreams in order to justify their decisions to give up on theirs, and don't let anyone talk you out of your dream. It's your dream, so only you can decide whether the risks and sacrifices are worth it.

21: Jessica "Evil" Eye

"Jessica Eye can fight. Jessica Eye is more than her past. Jessica Eye is forging her future."

The phrasing of this quote makes it clear what its purpose is: a mantra to focus and strengthen Jessica Eye through her toughest times.

As a perennial contender, she has spent most of her career fighting many of the toughest women in her division. She knows about fighting through adversity as well as anyone alive. Having a mantra like this to focus your mind is a great way to push through your struggles.

The power of a mantra is well known among those who practice meditation, and there is much scientific research backing up its benefits (though much more still needs to be done). The essential idea is that repeating a meaningful phrase over and over again while meditating can help the mind cleanse itself of negative thoughts and emotions.

Jessica Eye's use of her mantra to fortify her self-belief has kept her in the top ten of her division for nearly a decade.

22. Cris "Cyborg" Venancio

"I'm already used to being a target, so I'm building a castle with the stones people throw at me."

"Cyborg" has entered that rare and exclusive pantheon of fighters like Fedor and Cro Cop, who are so well known by their nicknames that people scarcely know what their real names are.

She got there in much the same way as well: by putting up such a string of legendary performances that she is thought of more as the embodiment of fighting spirit than as a mere mortal like the rest of us.

That said, being a woman in a male-dominated sport is a tough road, especially when "Cyborg" was in her prime at a moment when women's MMA was far less recognised and respected than it is today. This fact only makes her accomplishments all the more impressive.

Venancio's amazing spirit is well-illustrated by this beautiful quote. One can almost picture her lifting the stones herself and setting them in place on her castle walls before she ventures into the Octagon to dispatch another foe. Visualisation like this can help us use the words of naysayers to their opposite intended effect and make our belief in ourselves stronger than ever.

23. Max "Blessed" Holloway

"It's what kings do. If you want to be the best, you have to beat the best."

Max Holloway knows about beating the best. Not only has he overcome some legendary champions in Frankie Edgar and Anthony Pettis, but he also defeated one of the all-time contenders for the title of greatest pound-for-pound fighter, José Aldo, in order to win and then defend the UFC featherweight (145 lbs) championship in back-to-back matches.

Holloway's quote shows another aspect, and another value, of self-belief: relishing a challenge. When you believe in yourself strongly enough, you look for the most difficult imaginable goals. You don't settle for beating the mediocre–you don't compare yourself to the 'average'. If you believe you are a king, you set out to beat the best.

Holloway certainly did that, and he didn't find it easy either. He's dropped two fights to the larger Dustin Poirier and one to Conor McGregor. He has also found himself outwrestled and stifled to decision losses by the wrestling of both Denis Bermudez and Alexander Volkanovski. However, Holloway took every defeat in stride and answered them with wins against equally impressive competition. He wants to be the king and continues to sign bouts with the best, taking them to the limit, win or lose.

24. Stipe Miocic

"I like being the underdog. I like turning around and shutting people up when they tell me I can't."

Widely recognised as perhaps the greatest UFC heavyweight champion of all time, Stipe Miocic seems like a strange candidate to talk about enjoying the underdog status, but he was, in fact, considered the underdog in many of his great performances.

What makes Stipe so great are his straightforward technical skills, intelligent game-planning, discipline, and the self-belief to put them all together night after night. Most of the other great fighters, especially in the heavyweight division, seem more like forces of nature than Miocic, who, on the contrary, comes off as a humble everyman just doing his best.

Of course, as the quote shows, Miocic enjoys getting the chance to show that a humble everyman just doing his best can be the baddest man on the planet– and his quote also serves as a great reminder that you can use the words of naysayers and sceptics to energise yourself.

When anyone makes you feel like you can't do it, imagine how good Stipe felt after winning the UFC championship as a +165 underdog.

25. Joanna Jędrzejczyk

"I'm not cocky. I'm not arrogant. I know my value."

How common and tiring it must be for a celebrity to have positive self-belief confused with cockiness and arrogance. Joanna Jędrzejczyk is no stranger to this struggle: She's undeniably one of the greatest female MMA fighters of all time, with a dominant UFC strawweight (115 lbs) championship run that included five straight title defences.

During her reign, however, she got into a fair few trash-talking incidents and, after her reign, also had some fairly serious contract negotiation issues with the UFC. In both cases, detractors accused her of lacking an appropriate amount of humility. Joanna has never backed down, though, either in the ring or out of it. Knowing her value was what made her a champion, and she wasn't about to forget it over a few words.

Knowing your value isn't a matter of cockiness or arrogance. Cockiness is overestimating your value without putting in any work to have earned it; arrogance is believing that your value entitles you to look down on others. As long as you've earned your value and proved it with accomplishments, and you don't use it to look down on anyone else, you can disregard comments to the contrary and, like Joanna Jedrezjcyk, keep going on your own path to your dreams.

26. Dustin "The Diamond" Poirier

"Grit, determination, the right amount of crazy self-belief—everything it takes to be a champion. I have that."

Dustin Poirier's quote nicely sums up the theme of this whole chapter.

Notice what three things he lists as necessary to be a champion–all character traits. Not only that, but self-belief, "the right amount of crazy self-belief", is given particular emphasis. Why doesn't he mention talent or physical ability, considering that's the first and most obvious thing anyone would think of when it comes to being a champion fighter, or any kind of athlete for that matter?

A man like Poirier has met and trained with dozens if not hundreds of extremely talented, physically amazing people, and most of them will never be champions. The character traits he mentioned are rarer, and thus ultimately more important, than the physical traits we all mentally assume.

Poirier goes a little further than that, though. He not only considers "grit, determination, [and] the right amount of crazy self-belief" necessary to be a champion; he considers them sufficient to be a champion. He calls them "everything it takes to be a champion". How could someone with no physical ability ever become a champion fighter? Well, he didn't say champion fighter; he said champion.

If you have the right character traits, you can be a champion—or whatever the pinnacle of achievement may be called—in whatever field is appropriate for whatever talents you do have and choose to develop.

Chapter 2:

Commitment

Commitment is the foundation of any long-term progress towards a goal, and long-term progress is the only way to achieve the greatest and most ambitious goals we have.

It isn't easy to maintain commitment for the long haul. The world is always changing, as are we. As circumstances constantly shift, how are we supposed to know what we should stay committed to? Shouldn't we be flexible, open to new opportunities, and wary of wasting time and effort?

These are good questions to ask but beware of what you base your answers on.

Are you avoiding commitment because it's wise to be flexible, or simply because commitment can be tedious and challenging, and shiny new things are more fun and engaging?

There is never a one-size-fits-all answer to the hard questions of life. By looking to the great champions of MMA for their words on commitment and how to maintain it, we can learn the benefits that come from a life of dedication to help us find the answers we seek.

27. *"El Guapo" Bas Rutten*

"A true champion is one who sweats from exhaustion when no one is watching."

Bas Rutten, Pancrase and UFC champion, was sadly cut down in his prime by multiple simultaneous training injuries, prompting him to retire on doctor's orders in 1999. As a result, today's fight fans know him mainly as a funny, if knowledgeable commentator who used to be a respected fighter. What they perhaps don't know is that he retired with a 22-fight unbeaten streak, held multiple world titles, and was considered practically unbeatable.

What made Bas so feared? In a word: commitment.

As exemplified in this quote, Bas Rutten trained the hardest. In the 90s, almost all MMA stars came into the sport with a specific skill set from another established martial art and did their best to win with whatever skills they had. 'Cross training' was rare: kickboxers kickboxed, wrestlers wrestled, submission artists went for submissions, and the guy who got caught by the other guy's skill set first lost.

Rutten was one of the first fighters to break that mould; he had a background in kickboxing when he entered Pancrase, one of the first true MMA competitions in the world. After early struggles with the grappling of the catch wrestlers that dominated Pancrase, Rutten decided to get serious about his submission game. Within months he went from getting submitted himself to submitting experienced shoot wrestlers and BJJ black belts. His 22-fight unbeaten streak had begun.

Rutten's commitment to training the hardest to master every useful aspect of MMA made him perhaps the first truly dominant, true *mixed* martial arts fighter in the world.

28. Nate Diaz

"Whoever has lost a fight in the UFC and hasn't wanted to fight that guy the next day shouldn't be in the sport."

This quote from Nate Diaz shows the fighting spirit that made him and his brother Nick two of the most popular and successful MMA fighters of all time. Nobody has ever doubted their will to fight once the cage doors close, and even on the rare occasions that they were physically outmatched, their determination to keep coming forward until they win, or the bell rings has made them feared and respected opponents.

The Diaz brothers' fighting style can only be described as relentless pressure: always standing in range to hit and be hit, always throwing the first punch and the last punch, and always ready to score a TKO or submission finish when their tired and frustrated opponent slips up and makes one mistake.

How do the Diaz brothers pull this style off? Their commitment to their training regimen is the only explanation. Nobody has more cardio than them. They compete in triathlons for fun in between fights.

That is the kind of commitment that can make anyone great.

29. Miesha "Cupcake" Tate

"Failure isn't everything unless you just stop with that."

Miesha Tate truly lived the meaning of this quote.

She was committed to being the champion as, in her own words, "becoming a champion means more to me than anything—more than a rematch, more than anything".

With that as her focus, every fight she lost meant little more to her than the non-championship fights she won. All she cared about was winning the championship in the end, no matter how many losses it would take to get there.

She won the Strikeforce women's bantamweight (135 lbs) championship in 2011, but quickly lost it to Ronda Rousey. She rematched Rousey for the championship in the UFC, but lost again, and it seemed that her time as champion had come and gone. However, Tate never gave up, and after Rousey lost to Holly Holm, Tate was given another shot to take the belt, this time from Holm. In a career-defining, back-and-forth match, Tate finally submitted and defeated Holm in the fifth and final round, making her a champion in both Strikeforce and the UFC.

Tate suffered many defeats on her road to both titles, but her commitment to being the champion made those defeats little more than temporary setbacks. Her victories will last forever.

30. Georges "Rush" St. Pierre

"Every little thing you do leads up to a bigger thing."

This quote, by a man best known simply as "GSP", is an excellent motto to keep in mind when your daily grind seems hard, boring, and potentially pointless.

It was the little things that GSP did every day that added up to the "bigger thing" that is his life: the life of one of the greatest pound-for-pound fighters of all time. St. Pierre dominated what was considered possibly the toughest division in MMA, the UFC welterweight (170 lbs) division, for a decade.

From 2003 to 2013, GSP fought and beat the best fighters in the world (suffering only two losses which he quickly and emphatically avenged in rematches) and retired after holding the belt with a then-record breaking ten straight title defences. Just for good measure, GSP came back four years later to take the middleweight belt from Michael Bisping before retiring again.

What made GSP so special was his commitment to the gym. He was famously never not in shape. He maintained his commitment to his training even in retirement, which enabled him to come back and win a title fight after a four-year layoff. Georges St. Pierre is a man who always does the little things because he knows their value. For him, their value is a legacy that will endure in history for as long as MMA itself does.

What could we all accomplish if we committed to always doing the little things too?

31. Anderson "The Spider" Silva

"A champion is defined by the adversity he overcomes."

Anderson Silva will go down in history for the ease with which he demolished the UFC middleweight (185 lbs) division when he was in his prime. Still, he has also faced and overcome great adversity, both early in his career and towards its end.

It is the character and commitment he showed in overcoming his toughest struggles that made him a champion, even if fans remember him best for his easiest and most dominant wins.

One of Anderson Silva's early defeats was to Daiju Takase; despite having an overwhelming advantage on the feet, Silva fell into a triangle choke submission and was forced to tap out. Many years later in his career, at the height of his dominant run, Anderson Silva defended his belt with a rib injury against Chael Sonnen. He was unable to move effectively and was dominated for four straight rounds until, towards the end of the fifth round, Silva capitalised on the same mistake that had handed him one of his only ever career losses. He locked up Sonnen in the same triangle choke that he had once been forced to tap out from.

Silva didn't just overcome his adversity, he added it to his arsenal, and when he faced adversity again, he turned to the same weapon that he had once been defeated by. That's the power of commitment.

32. Randy "The Natural" Couture

"A lot of us lead relatively sedentary lifestyles, so you have to motivate yourself and force yourself to go to the gym and do active things. The folks that have figured it out found that thing that they love and made it a big part of their lives. It's easy for them to stay in shape."

Randy Couture isn't as well-known among current fans as he should be.

His personality has never been as flamboyant and attention-grabbing as some of his contemporaries like Tito Ortiz, and some unfortunate pay disputes resulted in him not getting the same kind of promotional push from the UFC as one of his biggest rivals, Chuck Lidell. Nevertheless, Couture's skills, accomplishments and longevity in the sport are more than sufficient to make him a legend.

Couture was the first man to hold a championship in two weight classes: heavyweight (265 lbs) and light heavyweight (205 lbs). He is, in total, a six-time champion. Perhaps the most amazing part of his story is that he won four of those belts when he was already over the age of 40. His last win came at the age of 47, making him the oldest fighter ever to win a UFC match.

Couture's reign is unique not just for his age but also because he always lived up to his nickname, "The Natural", by avoiding any PED (performance-enhancing drug) scandals. With this quote, he dispenses valuable and relatable advice: When you find a reason to stay in shape, when you find a way to love it, it's much easier. Forcing yourself to go to the gym to stay in shape is way tougher than loving it.

Commitment doesn't have to be a painful exercise in deprivation and self-discipline. If you try different things until you find something you love, you can make it much easier on yourself to be a lifelong 'natural' like the legendary Randy Couture.

33. Alistair "The Demolition Man" Overeem

"I go to bed with a clear conscience. I sleep great. I know I did my best."

Alistair Overeem is a true legend of MMA, having competed throughout Pride FC's heyday, placing highly in multiple Grand Prix tournaments, and claiming championships in Dream, Strikeforce, and even K-1. Although Overeem, now inactive and considering retirement, is unlikely to win a UFC championship to go along with all his other amazing accolades, he will sleep great for the rest of his life.

This quote says exactly why: when you do your best, you can go to bed with a clear conscience.

Somctimes, people can get stuck in a malaise of anxiety or regret without being able to pinpoint exactly why. It affects their sleep, their mood, and ultimately their ability to succeed at their biggest goals in life. One possible thing to try if you find yourself feeling this way is to simply choose something small and simple and just focus on doing your absolute best at that one thing. It could be a simple household chore, an aspect of your job or schooling, maybe a gift or favour for a loved one; whatever it is, if you can do it to the best of your ability, that might help clear your conscience, allow you to get a better night's sleep, and help give you some energy and confidence to accomplish your bigger goals as well.

34. Paige "12 Gauge" VanZant

"Keep working hard and find the areas you need to work on. See what you did wrong and work on it."

This is great, commonsense advice from a popular MMA star. Paige VanZant had a stellar early career, improving rapidly from almost no MMA experience at age 18 to competing at the highest levels of the UFC in her early 20s, steadily adding grappling, boxing, and kickboxing techniques to her repertoire between each hard-fought victory.

Her progress was somewhat derailed by nagging, repeated injuries and surgeries resulting from a poorly healed broken bone in her arm, but from the learning curve she demonstrated when she was healthy, VanZant is sure to be a force in her division for years to come.

The key to her success, particularly in adapting to the top level of the game so quickly after being thrown into the deep end so early on, is her commitment to constant improvement. Win or lose, "12 Gauge" systematically finds her mistakes and works to eliminate them.

You cannot do that without first being willing to try and to fail, and, secondly, being willing to commit to finding and working on whatever flaws are exposed by the challenges you take on, even though it's far easier to just sit back and be satisfied with whatever happens.

35. Valentina "Bullet" Shevchenko

"My understanding of the world is all through the prism of martial arts. It's affected every aspect of my life."

Here is another great quote from the amazing Valentina Shevchenko, which goes to show how her commitment to martial arts has bled through to positively impact everything she does.

It seems contradictory and counter-intuitive, but it's an interesting paradox that has held true for many people: the more committed they are to martial arts, or a similar self-discipline-based practice, the more well-rounded they become as individuals.

Shevchenko is a perfect example of this, as her martial arts accomplishments did not take away from anything else; on the contrary, as she says, they contributed to her ability to learn three languages and graduate from film school.

The wonderful thing about total commitment to a difficult discipline like martial arts is that it doesn't require you to give up other aspects of your life. It doesn't take time and energy away from other goals you might have. Instead, what you'll find is that your commitment to something like martial arts gradually increases your energy levels, motivation, self-discipline, and confidence, to the point that you accomplish more in other areas than you ever could have before, even counting the time and energy that you put into martial arts.

36. Dana White

"Anything can be changed. Anything can be fixed. Things that are broken can be fixed. And you don't have to be some billionaire or millionaire to do it. You just have to be a person with a vision and the passion to do it and be willing to fight for it every day."

The president of the UFC himself, Dana White, knows all about the power of a vision you have the passion to commit yourself to.

His early life was anything but easy—In fact, he was once visited and threatened by the mob in his hometown of Boston, which prompted him to leave for Las Vegas immediately.

In the year 2000, White was working as a manager for MMA stars Tito Ortiz and Chuck Liddell when he heard that Semaphore Entertainment Group was interested in putting the UFC up for sale. He contacted old friends Frank and Lorenzo Fertitta to see if they were interested in buying it, and the deal was done for 2 million dollars in January 2001, with Dana himself installed as president.

In the two decades since then, Dana White transformed the failing 2-million-dollar company into a more than 10-billion-dollar global juggernaut. Along the way, he has battled regulatory bodies, politicians, rival organisations, and even kept UFC going on Fight

Island in Abu Dhabi during the height of the Covid-19 Pandemic, to build up both the legitimacy and popularity of the UFC and of MMA in general.

While Dana White isn't a professional fighter like everyone else quoted in this book, it would be remiss not to acknowledge the incredibly important role his vision, passion and self-belief have played in developing the modern sport of MMA. There's hardly a better example anywhere of what you can accomplish with commitment to a vision over time.

37. Dustin "The Diamond" Poirier

"We fall, but we get up because the ground is no place for a champion."

Dustin Poirier's quote expresses a key concept of stoicism: the important questions of ethics are framed not around particular actions and moral quandaries, but rather around what kind of person one wants or should want to be.

As Dustin says, we get up after we fall because that's what a champion does.

Ethical systems, or life-guiding philosophies, are not so much comprehensive lists of things you should do under equally exhaustive lists of circumstances as they are a kind of personality that one should aim to adopt, and a kind of ideal one should strive to embody.

The ideal of a champion is someone who gets up because they know the ground is no place for them. The ideal of a champion is not someone who is never defeated, but someone who recovers from every defeat and rises again, wiser and stronger.

If you commit yourself to embodying the ideal of a champion, questions about what exactly you should do at what exact time under what exact circumstances won't bother you; all that you have to think about is embodying the ideal of a champion, and acting accordingly.

38. "Iron" Michael Chandler

"Hard work pays off if you're patient enough to see it through."

UFC lightweight (155 lbs) contender Michael Chandler hits on an important insight with this quote.

Plenty of people are willing to put in hard work—for a time. Then, when they don't see the hard work paying off, they start to think of it as a waste of time and effort and lose motivation to keep it up. The problem is that hard work takes time and patience to reap dividends.

Think of how useful a bridge is; now think of how useless 90% of a bridge is. It takes a lot of hard work to finish a bridge, but it's completely useless until it's done. A lot of things in life are like that, especially the most valuable things. You don't see the value in all the hard work you're doing until you've seen it all the way through.

One thing many MMA fighters have in common is that they got their start dedicating themselves to a martial art that ultimately went nowhere, then transitioning to MMA later. Michael Chandler started out as a high school and collegiate wrestler, a sport with almost no direct career prospects. Chandler never made the Olympics either. Do you think he considers the time and effort he put into wrestling a waste? Of course not, because that base has made him an excellent MMA fighter: ranked in the top five in one of the toughest divisions in the world, not to mention a multiple time Bellator champion.

His hard work absolutely paid off, even if it didn't pay off in the way he might have initially expected. So will yours if you have the patience to see it through.

39. Urijah "The California Kid" Faber

"This is the one sport you don't want to be one foot in one foot out."

Urijah Faber was a pioneer of his weight class, one of the biggest champions of the WEC and one of the men most responsible for promoting lower weight classes to mainstream prominence. His fight team, Team Alpha Male, is still responsible for turning out many of the top contenders at featherweight (145 lbs) and below.

In this quote, Faber makes an excellent point about the dangers of failing to fully commit. He naturally emphasises his own discipline, MMA, but there are, of course, plenty of other examples. Anything where the cost of failure is high, is something where commitment should not be taken lightly, and it turns out that that includes most things of true value.

Whether you're fighting, or teaching, or engineering, or building, or fixing, or caring for someone's health, or any number of other things, failing to commit adds to the risks of failure. While it's true that many quotes deal with recovering from failure and learning and moving on, one of the first things people often learn from failure is the cost of failing to fully commit; Urijah Faber's quote eloquently reminds us of that.

40. "Thug" Rose Namajunas

"Your mind is just like your body. It's a muscle you can train and get better at."

Rose Namajunas expresses one of the most important ideas in the psychology of self-improvement: that treating our mind as something we can improve with training and commitment works.

This idea stands in opposition to the pessimistic view that our minds, our intelligence, our personality traits, and so on, are determined from birth or early childhood, and that from then on, we are stuck with who we are. Rose Namajunas refused to believe that, and champions and successful people of all stripes are on the same side.

"Thug" Rose, like many champions, did not have it easy growing up. Her parents were very recent immigrants to the US when she was born, having just come from communist-controlled Lithuania. Rose grew up in a tough neighbourhood, and in her friend group, she was the smallest, but she got her nickname "Thug" because of her intimidating scowl and refusal to back down.

She is the first woman to win, lose, and then regain the UFC women's strawweight (115 lbs) championship, and she did it by always remaining unfazed, not only in the face of intimidating opponents like Joanna Jędrzejczyk, Jessica Andrade and Zhang Weili, but by also remaining unfazed by the memories of her own defeats. Her mind has always been her greatest strength because of the commitment she put into training it as well as her body.

41: Royce Gracie

"There is no age as long as the body feels good."

Royce Gracie, the near-mythical inaugural champion of the UFC, is the epitome of commitment.

As perhaps the most famous member of the famous Gracie family, Royce has always borne incredible pressure to perform, not just for himself but for his entire family's legacy. He was chosen to represent the family in the first UFC not because he was considered to be the strongest fighter, but precisely because he was not a particularly powerful and intimidating-looking fighter.

The Gracie family's goal in organising the first UFC and challenging fighters from all martial arts backgrounds was to show that their Gracie Jiu-Jitsu techniques were the most effective in a real fight–so effective that even an average-looking man like Royce could defeat much larger and stronger-looking opponents.

Royce didn't just prevail; he dominated. He then went on to defend his championship in UFC 2 and then retake it in UFC 4 after withdrawing from UFC 3 due to dehydration. How could Royce defeat skilled and much larger opponents like Ken Shamrock, Jason DeLucia and Dan Severn despite giving up so much weight? The only answer is his commitment to his art,

Gracie Jiu-Jitsu. He had prepared his entire life for those moments, so that when they came, he was ready.

Now Gracie Jiu-Jitsu, or Brazilian Jiu-Jitsu in general, is widely regarded as an essential pillar of fighting techniques. Everyone now knows that while jiu-jitsu may not always win fights against trained opponents on its own, a lack of jiu-jitsu will certainly lose you the fight. That critical advancement of knowledge and technique in MMA is all thanks to the commitment of the Gracie family, especially its UFC champion, Royce Gracie.

42: Joanna Jędrzejczyk

"You know why I'm so confident? Because I am working so hard every day. That's why I am different than the other fighters and my opponents and challengers. That's why."

This quote, the second to be included in this book by the ever-intimidating Joanna Jędrzejczyk, perfectly combines the themes of chapters one and two. It not only expresses her unquestionable self-belief, but it also shows its source.

There's no better way to gain confidence in any kind of competitive scenario than to be confident that you have put the work in and made the commitment to do the best you can. You can't control whether or not you're naturally more gifted than your opponent. You certainly can't control whether or not you'll get luckier than your opponent. The only thing you can certainly control is your own level of commitment to being the best.

When you can be confident that your commitment is unmatched, that nobody out there is more dedicated than you are, that's when your confidence becomes truly justified and legitimate.

Joanna Jędrzejczyk is known not only for her great accomplishments, like being the first Polish UFC champion, but for her aggressive demeanour towards her opponents. She doesn't just beat them down in the

Octagon; she makes sure they know they're in for a beatdown every chance she gets.

This quote explains why she has that confidence. She's so sure she's the hardest worker that she considers victory an almost foregone conclusion—if not in this fight, then surely the next. Her commitment has made her not just a champion, but a perennial title threat even when she isn't holding the belt.

For anyone who wants that kind of confidence, commitment is the way to get it.

43. Dominick "The Dominator" Cruz

"Loss is part of life. If you don't have loss, you don't grow."

Dominick Cruz has always been thought of as a cerebral fighter, and philosophical quotes like this have done as much to reinforce that impression outside of the Octagon as his intelligent game-planning, and unorthodox fighting style has inside the Octagon.

Here, Cruz expresses a fundamental truth of life that can be found on every level. Muscle cells only grow back stronger when they are damaged by hard exertion, and, by the same token, lessons are often only learned when a loss exposes the mistakes and weaknesses that need to be corrected.

Cruz's career trajectory is another level on which we can observe the truth of this quote. Cruz started off dominant, earning his nickname with a 9-0 run before losing his first fight to fellow legend of the sport Urijah Faber. Cruz took the lessons of that loss to heart and went on another winning streak that culminated with him taking and defending the WEC and then UFC Bantamweight (135 lbs) belt, as well as avenging his only loss to Urijah Faber.

Despite a string of injuries causing extended layoffs that forced him to give up his championship belt, Cruz has been able to win back his title and remain in strong title contention whenever he's healthy enough to fight. How has he done this? Commitment to overcoming loss and growing from it is an essential ingredient of Cruz's success.

44. Chuck "The Iceman" Liddell

"A fighter with heart will almost always win out against a fighter with skill but no will."

Chuck Liddell, another true legend of the sport, emphasises the value of 'heart' with this quote.

In some ways, this echoes the sentiment of the earlier quote by Dustin Poirier: that your character is the key to success. In fighting, 'heart' can refer to a fighter's toughness, will to win and ability to absorb punishment without slowing down or backing off.

In that sense, the adage in boxing that "you don't want to be known for your heart" makes more sense because it implies that you tend to get beat up a lot in your fights. Liddell certainly passed that test with some grueling come-from-behind wins in his famous fights with Randy Couture and Alistair Overeem. However, Liddell is referring to a lot more than that when he talks about how "a fighter with heart almost always win[s] against a fighter with skill but no will".

What Liddell is also talking about in this quote is commitment: commitment to a lifestyle of hard training, day in and day out. His trainer, John Hackleman, is famous for pioneering the emphasis of physical conditioning and live sparring over karate kata, way back in 1986, long before MMA was brought to the mainstream by the UFC. This is what Liddell means by 'heart' over "skill but no will"; a karate practitioner in the 1980s could be considered extremely skilled by the speed and precision with which they executed kata, but would still have little chance in an actual fight with a fighter who committed to training their 'heart' with hard cardio training and live sparring.

This gives us a valuable insight into the role that willingly putting yourself into difficult situations can have in developing commitment.

45. Gina Carano

"When I enjoy doing something, I don't mind if it hurts."

Gina Carano is one of the first great women's MMA fighters and, along with Ronda Rousey, perhaps one of the most responsible for propelling it into the mainstream.

What made Carano unique among fighters was her friendly, disarming demeanour; looking at her beaming smile, one doesn't immediately imagine a fierce fighter lurking beneath that facade.

Even this quote, which certainly has an edge, was delivered with a broad grin.

However, Carano was never anything but business in the cage. She compiled a 7-0 record using ruthless Muay Thai skills to run through fighters that looked at least a little more intimidating at first glance than she did. Whatever punishment she took in her victories, it didn't faze her, and this quote explains why.

Commitment is something that takes discipline and something that needs to be developed. But when you find something you enjoy, it doesn't have to be a burden. On the contrary, getting yourself into a position where you can commit to something you love is in many ways halfway down the road to an ideal life—

or at least as close to ideal as most of us can reasonably expect.

Carano's quote reminds us that pain is in our mind; when we are doing something that's worth it, pain hurts less, but when we are doing something we already hate, a paper cut can feel like a severed finger. Find what you love, commit to it, and you may find you can live a life where you don't mind so much when something hurts.

46. Amanda "Lioness" Nunes

"I started my career with a loss, getting 'slapped' by life."

Amanda Nunes comes from a family of fighters: her mother was a boxer, and her uncle fought in Vale Tudo. She trained in martial arts from the time she was five, beginning with *capoeira*, then advancing to karate, boxing, Brazilian jiu-jitsu and MMA by the time she was 16. She slept on the mats of the gym and, despite being the only woman, dominated her training partners. She seemed destined for a successful career in MMA, but her first fight didn't go as planned as she was submitted by arm bar.

In spite of this inauspicious beginning, Nunes was already committed, so she took the loss in her stride, learned, and moved on. She would be defeated three more times on her way up the rankings, but her commitment and dedication never wavered. After her last loss, to Cat Zingano, Nunes went on a 12-fight winning streak–and counting. She captured both the UFC women's featherweight (145 lbs) and bantamweight (135 lbs) championships, and has held and defended both belts simultaneously, the only UFC fighter ever to do so.

She is widely considered the best pound-for-pound women's MMA fighter of all time. And it all started with commitment: a commitment that one, two, even four losses could not break.

47. Nick Diaz

"You got to love it, so you want it so bad that you're pushing yourself to those limits that you hate it."

Nick Diaz is one of the most popular stars of the sport.

It's not just because he's a great fighter, and it's not just because every match he's had has been an amazing fight (win or lose), though all that certainly helps. Diaz is also known for his famous love-hate relationship with fighting, which he expresses beautifully in this quote.

Diaz has famously complained about many aspects of fighting, from the fact that he feels forced by the fight game to bear ill will towards men he otherwise would have no problem with, to the fact that he hates doing media appearances, and even down to the simple fact that fighting can be a brutal, painful activity, and he has expressed a wish that he could make as much money just doing triathlons or something else.

However, deep down, Nick Diaz is as pure a fighter as you can find anywhere. He loves it, and he loves it so bad that he pushes himself to those limits where he hates it. He doesn't always like to admit it, but it slips out in quotes like this one from time to time, and it shines forth as obvious as the sun on a cloudless day when Diaz is in the ring, standing in the pocket, taunting his opponent with his arms straight out, then landing his signature 'Stockton Slap' to counter everything the opponent tries to throw.

If you can find something you love so bad that you push yourself until you hate it, that's the kind of commitment that makes such an arresting superstar like Nick Diaz.

48. Urijah "The California Kid" Faber

"Good health is true wealth."

Urijah Faber channels his inner Benjamin Franklin with this bit of punchy rhyming wisdom.

He makes a great point too.

There's almost nothing that could cost you more over the long run of your life than poor health, and almost nothing more valuable than good health. Good health is the foundation upon which most other success depends. As Confucius once said, "A healthy man wants 1000 things, a sick man only wants one."

Good health is more than just good physical health, too; good mental health is equally important, and they are so tightly linked that it's not like you ever have to choose anyway. Everything you do to make your body healthier, from good sleep to good diet and exercise, will also make your mind healthier. Likewise, a strong mind is an essential ingredient to the kind of commitment you need to maintain a healthy body well into old age.

Speaking of wealth, many of us think of retirement in terms of saving up our wealth to sustain ourselves. But a wealthy retirement does not last long or enjoyably unless it's also a healthy retirement. Don't only think of saving your money for retirement; think also of saving your health. Just as every bit of money you save from your paycheck can result in big dividends from compound interest, so too will the exercise, diet and sleep habits that you maintain pay big dividends for your long-term health. You will need both because, as Faber says, "Good health is true wealth".

49. Stipe Miocic

"I just work hard at everything I do. If there's something I need to learn, I stick to it, I learn it and put everything I have toward it."

Stipe Miocic demonstrates the kind of commitment that has made him one of MMA's greatest heavyweight champions with this quote.

Sometimes, life is extremely complicated; but sometimes, it's a lot simpler than we make it out to be. Sometimes, life is as simple as just working hard at everything you do, focusing on what you need to learn to get past your next challenge, and putting everything you have toward it until it's accomplished.

Stipe's words hint at what that kind of commitment takes: focus, on one thing at a time.

Here's a simple three-step process to accomplishing your dreams: pick something great and aim at it; move towards it until something stops you or slows down; focus on whatever that is, work on learning whatever you need to learn to get around it, and stick to it until it's done. Then, you just keep moving until the next thing in your way appears. Do that for a lifetime, and there's no telling what you might accomplish.

In Stipe's case, he's already won multiple UFC heavyweight championships, and he's not done yet.

50. Miesha "Cupcake" Tate

"Make excuses to work out. Go for walks and enjoy the scenery. You'd be surprised how many calories you can burn during the day if you just make an effort and become more aware. Also, remember to start slow, don't go into it too hard if you are just starting."

With her second quote on commitment, Miesha Tate dishes out some great, common-sense advice for anyone looking to stay healthy.

The key to incorporating more exercise into your daily life is to make excuses to do it and be more aware and mindful. She talks about how easy it is to burn a surprising number of calories by being more aware.

Some examples could be to take the stairs instead of the elevator or escalator, to park farther away from the entrances of shopping centres, so you get to walk more or to carry more groceries instead of using a shopping cart for everything. And of course, like Miesha says in her quote, go for walks and enjoy the scenery. A nice walk or run is a great way to enjoy your favourite podcast or music too.

We can't all be MMA champions, but we can all be healthy, happy, and successful. Start small and start slow, but keep going, stay committed to a healthy lifestyle, and you'll reap exponential rewards over time.

51. Khabib "The Eagle" Nurmagomedov

"Win or lose, I believe in giving my best, and that is what I do."

Here is another simple, yet profound piece of wisdom from Khabib Nurmagomedov.

Of course, Khabib never lost in his professional career, but this quote seems to hint that although the possibility of losing has occurred to him, it hasn't bothered him. It shouldn't bother us either. In a zero-sum competition like MMA, for every winner, there must be a loser, and on a long enough timeline, we're sure to be on the losing end sooner or later. Whenever you do lose, there's no regret if you gave your best, and there's every opportunity to learn from whatever went wrong and determine how to avoid or overcome it in the future.

True commitment is the closest we ordinary mortals can get to a superpower. It's more empowering than wealth and more important than talent. Commitment is what makes champions. Commitment is the power of compound interest; every day, you sacrifice a little bit of energy and time to your long-term goals, and every day the results compound, until you're an unstoppable force. The hard part of commitment is the same as the hard part of saving up for retirement: the sacrifice seems big, and the gains seem tiny. But every day that you stay committed, it keeps compounding.

Pick a path and keep that momentum going until you're living the life you've always dreamed and keeping it up is easy and natural.

Chapter 3:

Fear

Fear is an omnipresent part of a fighter's life.

In ancient Greece, Ares, the god of war, was accompanied by Deimos, the god of dread, and Phobos, the god of fear and panic. Deimos was believed to weaken Ares' opponents before battle by making them dread it, and Phobos was thought to drive his enemies into panic and disorder during the battle.

Alexander the Great mastered these fears by famously making great sacrifices to Phobos before the battle of Gaugamela, and sure enough, Darius III, emperor of Persia, fled the field. The Spartans also worshipped Phobos, constructing a great shrine to him and believing that fear held the state together.

There are few things more fearsome in the modern world than stepping into a ring or Octagon and facing down someone who intends to hurt you as much as necessary to win the fight.

However, it's not so much the pain the fighters fear; it's more that fighters always know in the back of their minds how much is riding on each match. Fighters generally have to win to get a bonus that pays their training camp expenses. They also have to win to advance their careers and move up the rankings to challenge for a title match and improve their negotiating position for future contracts.

Deep down, every fighter must wonder if they're really good enough to be champion, and if this career is really worth pursuing if they aren't.

Above all, fighters need to avoid serious injury. A blown-out knee, a repeatedly broken hand, a detached retina–these injuries and more have derailed the careers of great fighters in their prime. Then what? You've spent your whole life dedicating yourself to a career you can no longer participate in because of two seconds of bad luck; you may never get back in the Octagon, but you still have a family to support and bills to pay, and now you have no way to pay them. What could be more frightening than that?

Every weekend, fighters face these fears and more, and every time they step in the cage, nod their head, tap their gloves, and then move to the centre of the Octagon, they defeat them. How do they do it and make it look so easy?

This chapter looks at some quotes from some of MMA's greatest fighters to seek insight and inspiration on facing our fears.

52. Rickson Gracie

"Our fears don't stop death. They stop life."

This quote from Rickson Gracie is beautiful in its simplicity and power.

Rickson immediately cuts to the heart of the problem: we evolved a sense of fear to keep ourselves alive, but we also understand on some level that death will come for us all sooner or later.

No matter how fearful you may be, and no matter how careful that makes you, you won't live forever. Nobody will. So, at that point, what are your fears really accomplishing? It's not nothing—it's worse than nothing. They're stopping you from truly living. Your fears cannot save you from death, not forever. But they can immediately stop you from living the kind of life you'd wish for yourself if you had the courage to embrace it.

Rickson Gracie overcomes his fear by twisting it around on itself. His words don't teach us that there's nothing to fear, because that would be a lie. There's plenty to fear. The thing to fear most of all is failing to live the life of your dreams out of fear. In other words, to borrow from and update a famous quote of President Franklin Delano Roosevelt, it's not so much that "there's nothing to fear but fear itself", but rather, "there's nothing to fear more than fear itself".

It takes ignorance of danger to fear nothing, but the wise can overcome the fear of danger by measuring it against the greater fear of regret—regret that cowardice will stop us from living.

53. "Rowdy" Ronda Rousey

"People say to me all the time, 'You have no fear'. I tell them, 'No, that's not true. I'm scared all the time. You have to have fear in order to have courage. I'm a courageous person because I'm a scared person.'"

Ronda Rousey was perhaps the single most important figure in bringing women's MMA into the mainstream.

She demolished her outmatched opponents with her Olympic-level Judo skills, racking up a string of very fast victories, all by arm bar, until claiming both Strikeforce and UFC gold in the bantamweight (135 lb) division.

With this quote, Rousey reminds us of what courage really means. It doesn't mean the absence of fear, ignorance of danger, or pure foolhardiness. Courage means knowing your fear, understanding it, and setting it aside to do what you have to do. You cannot have courage merely by not knowing or understanding you're in danger; it's only when you understand, you feel that fear, and then you overcome it anyway, that you're truly brave.

Rousey never showed any fear, though she certainly had it. She knew all along that any fight could be her last, but she was determined to go out and do her job anyway. She proved her courage when she came back from a devastating knockout loss to Holly Holm to challenge perhaps the most fearsome and dominant woman in MMA history, Amanda Nunes, and though she was badly outmatched on the feet, she kept coming forward anyway.

54. Brian "T-City" Ortega

"I very strongly dislike fear. I always say fear keeps us from living our lives and doing the things we want to do."

Brian Ortega, UFC featherweight (145 lbs) contender, echoes much of the sentiment of Rickson Gracie's quote (number 52) above.

It has the same message that fear is what keeps people from living life to the fullest and doing all the things they want to do.

The wording gives it a slightly different twist, though, perhaps owing to Ortega's different personality. He isn't the philosopher-fighter that Rickson Gracie is, raised in a legendary martial arts family to carry forward his family's honour. Ortega is the son of Mexican immigrants, raised in California, and got his start at fighting in kickboxing. The Gracie influence on his outlook makes sense, though; he started training Gracie Jiu-Jitsu under Rorion Gracie in his teens.

Ortega's quote hints at how he chooses to deal with his fear: He simply dislikes it, very strongly. One might even say that he gets angry at his fear and uses that anger to squash it.

This is well attested to by how he fights: ferociously, always looking for the finish, and even when he comes up short, as in his first two title shots, he frequently comes away with a Fight of the Night bonus as a consolation. There are those who say that anger hides fear, as if that's necessarily a weakness. Well, everyone feels fear, and if anger is what helps you get past it, so what?

There are times when anger can be a liability, of course, but anger, like all emotions, can be controlled. If you find it easier to control your anger than your fear, using your anger to overcome it just makes good sense.

55. "The Notorious" Conor McGregor

"I am comfortable in the uncomfortable."

Conor McGregor certainly lives up to his nickname with notorious exploits in and out of the Octagon and ring.

While he's certainly a naturally gifted fighter, it's his gifts for chaos and charisma that have made him one of MMA's all-time biggest superstars.

After storming the MMA world with a big winning streak that took him all the way to an 11-second knockout win over the legendary José Aldo for the UFC featherweight (145 lbs) title, McGregor has cashed in on his fame with title fights, big money grudge matches, and even a pay-per-view boxing match in which he put up a respectable performance against all-time-great Floyd "Money" Mayweather.

McGregor's quote demonstrates another unique take on facing your fear: remember that the other guy has to face his fear too. When you are put in an uncomfortable situation, you're often not alone. Sometimes, especially in any kind of competitive endeavour, the other guy has every reason to be just as uncomfortable as you are. If you can bear this in mind like McGregor does, you can turn that discomfort into your own advantage.

McGregor thrives on making his opponents uncomfortable; he antagonises them before and during matches, makes wild boasts and threats, and uses every psychological trick in the book. He purposefully makes the fight as uncomfortable as possible, and that puts him in control over the situation. When he knows that his opponent is even more uncomfortable than he is, he is able to be comfortable in the uncomfortable.

The lesson here is that you don't even have to stop at overcoming your fears; you can oftentimes find opportunities to take control of fearsome circumstances and turn them around. You can then become comfortable in the uncomfortable.

56. Max "Blessed" Holloway

"Don't be scared to look for help. Depression is real....It's crazy, and all these guys, us athletes, that keep thinking we're superheroes. I like to think I'm a superhero, but superheroes got to fight their demons too sometimes."

Max Holloway demonstrates a surprising bit of strength with this quote about being unafraid to show some vulnerability.

This quote is, in many ways, proof that vulnerability is not synonymous with weakness. On the contrary, hiding or covering up vulnerability often is a sign of weakness, especially if you're doing it to yourself.

The first step towards true strength is acknowledging your vulnerabilities. The common habit of willfully ignoring one's own vulnerabilities is what eventually turns them into true weaknesses over time. Facing them head-on is often not just the best way to deal with your struggles, but, in many cases, it's the only way.

By the same token, asking for help to deal with problems isn't a weakness at all–in fact, it's proof of one's strength. This is because no person is truly alone and fully independent; we are all in interdependent relationships with our families, friends, and communities at large. The ability to ask for help is proof that you have people in your life who can help you.

Far from that being a weakness, that's evidence of strength. A person is not limited to their own capacity to deal with problems; a person has the capacity of everyone they know that's willing to help when asked. Likewise, having people that are willing to help if asked is evidence of their belief in your capacity to help them or anyone they care about in turn.

We are not solitary creatures. We are social, communal creatures, and being willing to use the resources not just of ourselves but of everyone with a social bond to us is what makes us strong.

57. Nate Diaz

"If you don't find time to meditate and get all that negative out, and if you don't have the right people being positive around you, this is a very scary job to have if you don't learn how to control your fear."

Nate Diaz, the younger Diaz brother, packs a lot of very practical wisdom about fear into this quote.

The beginning of the quote lays out a couple of common ways of dealing with fear.

The first is finding the time to meditate to release negative emotions. Mindfulness meditation has a proven track record of success in reducing the impact of negative intrusive thoughts and feelings, including fear. By engaging in mindfulness meditation, one gains the ability over time to spot fear coming instantly, to acknowledge it and consider its utility in dealing with the present circumstances, and then to dismiss it and just let it go once it's served its purpose and is no longer helpful.

The second helpful way of dealing with fear is surrounding yourself with positive people who will share your burdens and lighten them with sympathy and encouragement. You can take a lot of strength from those who believe in you. Knowing that they will still have your back and think no less of you, win, or lose, can give you a ton of comfort, which can help relieve you of fears of negative consequences.

58. Paige "12 Gauge" VanZant

"You don't know your value until you test it."

This deceptively simple quote from Paige VanZant contains some deep wisdom.

In order to fully understand what she means; we have to consider all the meanings and usages of 'value'.

The most basic material understanding of the word is value to employers: in other words, what salary or wages you can demand. In this case, her quote means that you don't know how much you can demand to be paid until you go looking for several jobs and see how much you get offered. In many ways, just doing that can take an act of courage, as obviously, many employers would prefer their employees refrain from testing their value on the marketplace.

On a deeper level, your value can mean your own personal self-esteem and self-respect. In that case, testing your value means putting yourself into difficult, even fearsome situations, and then doing your best to come out on top. It's critical for our self-respect to test ourselves in this way at least occasionally; otherwise, deep down, we'll always wonder what we're really worth when the chips are down, and the situation is tough and scary.

The best part about testing your value is that even if you don't succeed in what you're challenging yourself at, you still won, because the real test was to see if you had the courage to make an honest attempt in the first place.

59. Robert "Bobby Knuckles" Whittaker

"Come fight night, there will be nerves, but it's how you react to those nerves—doing what you need to regardless—that's how you win fights."

"Bobby Knuckles", as he's affectionately known by his very loyal fan base in his birth country of New Zealand and around the world, has amply demonstrated his courage throughout his career.

Fighting in the stacked UFC middleweight (185 lbs) division, he's taken on a who's who of absolute killers. He's made a name for himself by never compromising his high-pressure style, even against numerous opponents famous for their vicious counter-striking or grappling styles like Israel Adesanya, Ronaldo Souza and Yoel Romero, who he defeated to claim the interim UFC middleweight championship in 2017.

His quote reiterates that nerves are an inescapable fact of life. Every time something important is on the line, you can't help but care about succeeding, and the more you care, the more you worry about things going wrong. The best ways to overcome these nerves include techniques like mindfulness meditation, visualisation, and preparation and training.

Deep down, the biggest source of worry is often worrying about regrets; if you've done everything you can to put yourself in a position to succeed, then, win or lose, you won't have regrets, so your biggest source of nerves will already be taken care of.

60. Georges "Rush" St. Pierre

"Fear is the genesis of most of the good things that have occurred in my life. Fear is the beginning of every success I've lived."

Georges St. Pierre has lived multiple lifetimes worth of successes already by any normal standard, so he is certainly qualified to talk about it.

It's interesting what a positive spin "Rush" can put on fear with this, his second quote in this book. He chooses to focus on the opportunity that accompanies fear, so for him, fear is little more than a sign pointing the way towards what he needs to do to achieve greater success.

With such a positive mindset, fear can be consistently overcome.

Your first fears are often the scariest and the hardest to face. The nice thing is that once you do, you get better at it. The more fears you overcome to achieve success, the more your fears start to look to you like they do to GSP. True champions don't fear their fears. They seek them out, using them as signs that there are new successes to be gained on the other side of that fear.

Once you find yourself willingly seeking out opportunities to experience new fears, you'll know you're really on the road to living your best life.

Chapter 4:

Positive Thinking

"The power of positive thinking" has almost become a cliché, but something usually only becomes a cliché when it's true.

The difficulty is in finding new ways to explain and apply that truth so that it doesn't become stale and bland. Fortunately, some of MMA's greatest champions can do even better than explain it–they can demonstrate it, from their own life experiences.

Many of the world's greatest fighters come from difficult circumstances: sometimes they have family problems, financial problems, or social problems, and sometimes they have all of the above and more. From those difficult circumstances, they rose to the pinnacle of stardom and success.

How did they do it? One of the earliest and best predictors of success is the ability to take control over your thoughts and emotions before they take control over you.

Understanding the principle of how to gain mastery over your thoughts and feelings is one of the core benefits of mindfulness meditation. Interestingly, it's also a core benefit of practising martial arts. Training in a martial art doesn't just involve training your body and physical skills. Doing the techniques repeatedly, mindfully, deliberately, through mounting exhaustion and under increasing pressure, requires a discipline of your mind that's very similar to discipline gained through mindfulness meditation.

It is the fighters who master that ability early on who often tend to have the most success.

It is a cliché that mental strength is as important as physical strength when it comes to winning in sports, but the quotes in this chapter from some of the world's greatest fighters can shed light on exactly how and why that is, and that can help us all learn how to succeed in our challenges in life.

61. "The Notorious" Conor McGregor

"At the end of the day, you have to feel some way. So why not feel invincible? Why not feel untouchable? Why not feel like the best to ever do it?"

Conor McGregor makes an excellent implied point with this question.

The obvious point is that if you could choose how to feel about yourself, the best way to feel, when heading into a competition at least, is to feel invincible, unbeatable, and the best ever.

The benefits of these feelings have already been well covered in chapter one.

The subtler, implied point is that we *can*, in fact, choose how we feel about ourselves. This isn't just some idle hypothesis; people can and do take control over how they feel about themselves.

There are a few different proven ways to do this.

One way is mindfulness meditation. Another is hard training in a martial art, which carries similar meditative and disciplining benefits.

Whichever way you get started down the path, you'll know you've ended up there when you can acknowledge negative self-talk, pessimistic thoughts, fears, and doubts, and simply let them go without them bothering or affecting you, and then replacing those thoughts with empowering, optimistic, motivational thoughts.

It takes a lot of work to get to this point, and the effort you put into taking control over your thoughts will slowly but surely be rewarded, as long as you stick with it over the long run.

62. "Rowdy" Ronda Rousey

"A loss leads to victory, being fired leads to a dream job…I find comfort in believing that good things can grow out of tragedy."

Ronda Rousey gives a great example of one of the best aspects of positive thinking: the belief that even the worst-case scenario will ultimately have a positive outcome. When you can believe that it will reduce your fears, and the ability to act fearlessly is a huge advantage in any difficult situation.

When your mind gets stuck focusing on worst-case outcomes, you can easily fall victim to a psychological phenomenon known as 'target fixation'. Target fixation is the paradoxical tendency of drivers and pilots to focus so much on what they want to avoid that it actually makes them more likely to collide with it. This is the cause of many accidents on the road, but, on a more abstract level, it's also the cause of many failures in people's lives. They become so worried about the negative possibilities that they freeze up, second-guess themselves, hesitate, and generally underperform relative to their true abilities when it matters most.

Being able to visualise positive long-term outcomes even in the face of short-term failure is one great way to help overcome those negative tendencies.

Rousey has faced defeat a few times in her life, but her positive thinking is justified by the superior outcomes she always moved on to afterwards. Her biggest defeats early on were in judo, where she was forced to settle for Olympic bronze, but she followed that up with championship runs in Strikeforce and the UFC. Then, when she lost her belt in the UFC, she followed that up with a championship run as one of the top stars of the WWE.

Rousey's career trajectory shows that good has the potential to follow bad so long as you stay positive and keep moving forward.

63. Darren "The Gorilla" Till

"I don't ever want to be inspired by someone else. I want to be inspired by myself."

One might easily assume Darren Till is hoping to follow in Bisping's footsteps and become another great striking-based MMA champion from England, but this quote shows how Till's thinking is different.

He's not hoping to follow in anyone's footsteps or live in anyone's shadow or, as he clearly puts it, "to be inspired by [anyone] else" besides himself. He is out there to forge his own path to greatness.

Like most fighters, Till's early life was hard. He trained in Muay Thai and kickboxing from a young age, and went pro very early, but struggled a lot in his personal life in Liverpool, ultimately getting kicked out of his mother's home and even getting into an altercation at a club in which he was stabbed in the back and was lucky to survive. Following that incident, Till moved to Brazil to continue training in a new environment, and stayed for three years.

Darren Till fought 11 times in Brazil and once in Argentina, winning every match, before getting the call to the UFC. He then extended his unbeaten streak to a total of 17, including very impressive victories over Donald "Cowboy" Cerrone and Stephen Thompson before finally meeting his match in then UFC welterweight (170 lbs) champion Tyron Woodley and then losing to Jorge Masvidal.

Till moved up to middleweight (185 lbs)–a weight he has had a much easier time making consistently–and has been a top contender there, defeating Kelvin Gastelum and losing only to Robert Whittaker and Derek Brunson.

Till's journey to inspire himself is not yet over. If he keeps up thinking positively, he may yet match Bisping's accomplishments—but don't put it to him that way. He's only looking to himself for inspiration.

64. Dan "The Hangman" Hooker

"Life's short. Smile while you still have teeth!"

Dan Hooker is another great MMA fighter from New Zealand, a UFC lightweight (155 lbs) contender with an aggressive, exciting style and a unique way with words. This quote perfectly sums up his attitude to fighting and certainly brings a smile to one's face, whether you still have teeth or not.

Like all funny quotes, it has its truth and wisdom to it too. Life may be short, but that's no reason not to enjoy it while you have it—in fact, it's even more reason to do so.

Dan Hooker addresses an existential question that deep down we generally prefer to avoid rather than face head-on: the realities not just of our own mortality, but of our own frailty. We will not always be healthy, young, and fit. We will not always have all our teeth with which to smile, or strong bodies with which to fight or even strong minds. There will come a time when everything we have fades away, and eventually, we will too.

Dan Hooker reminds us to make the most of the time that we do have. To smile while we still have teeth, to fight and to work and to strive and to succeed while we still have our health, and to love while we still have our friends and families.

Life is short, so don't waste it with negative thinking.

65. "Iron" Michael Chandler

"Life is too short and too sweet to complain about the silly things."

Following on from the previous quote very appropriately is "Iron" Michael Chandler, a man who defeated Dan Hooker in his UFC debut to gain his first UFC title shot.

Chandler's background as an American wrestler could hardly be more different from Dan Hooker, the New Zealand born kickboxer, but his outlook turns out to be extremely similar. Clearly, facing our own mortality with a positive outlook is a winning formula.

Humans generally tend to have a negativity bias. However, the world today is not nearly so harsh as it was for most of our biological history as humans, let alone as animals. Negativity bias today is holding us back and making us miserable far more than we need to be. Focusing on the positive doesn't come naturally and easily to most people, but it's better for us in the long run.

Chandler's ability to focus on the positive and let the negative slide made him a multiple time Bellator champion and have made him a top contender in the UFC lightweight (155 lbs) division as well. One way to help yourself focus on the positive is hinted at in this quote when Chandler mentions the sweetness of life in contrast to the silly things. It is the purposeful practice of gratitude: Every time you find yourself dwelling on a negative thing that's happened or even complaining about it out loud, take a moment to contrast it with everything you have to be grateful for, with everything in your life that's sweet.

Getting into the habit of self-directing your own thoughts away from the negative and towards the positive is a great way to get started on genuinely improving your life.

66. Cláudia Gadelha

"It's all about energy. If your energy is good, everything around you will be good also."

Cláudia Gadelha had a rough start in life, getting mixed up with the wrong kind of friends and getting involved with drugs.

To make matters worse, although she had a passion for martial arts ever since seeing a women's MMA match as a child, her parents didn't much care for the idea of her becoming a fighter.

However, to get her away from drugs, her parents took her to Natal, and she began training MMA on her own time at Natal's Kimura Nova União MMA club. The experience of training changed her life completely. At 18, she moved to Rio De Janeiro to train with José Aldo and make her professional MMA debut. A string of victories got her into the UFC, where she has been a UFC strawweight (115 lbs) contender since 2014.

Training in martial arts really changed Gadelha's life. She has been not only a major UFC star, fighting for the championship and winning multiple bonuses for Fight of the Night and Performance of the Night, but she is also working on a law degree in order to join the Brazilian special forces.

As her quote above says, if your energy is good, everything around you will be good also. Cláudia learned how to improve her energy with martial arts training, and now everything for her is good.

67. Michelle "The Karate Hottie" Waterson

"Through adversity, we find our better self."

Michelle Waterson is one of the pioneers and earliest stars of women's MMA, but unlike many pioneers, her career did not fade as the sport became more mainstream.

On the contrary, she continued to evolve and improve even as the level of competition drastically rose, which has allowed her to remain a top ten contender well over a decade after her professional debut.

What's even more impressive is that she is a natural atomweight (105 lbs) fighter and won her first championship there, but after joining the UFC, she has had to fight at strawweight (115 lbs) due to the UFC not having an atomweight division, which means that most of her opponents are naturally larger than her.

As this quote shows, Waterson has kept her thinking on the positive side. She knows that fighting the top fighters in the world, fighters like Rose Namajunas and Joanna Jędrzejczyk, is signing up for some serious adversity, but she isn't out for an easy ride. She's out to find her better self, and only by willingly seeking out adversity can we find that.

This isn't to say that all adversity is necessarily good, but Michelle Waterson is talking about voluntarily seeking out challenges, and willingly putting yourself in a tough spot. That kind of adversity, when you're properly physically and mentally prepared, is what brings out your best. And after all, it's far better to seek out tough times on your own terms, ready and willingly, than it is to sit back and try to enjoy an easy life until tough times find you, unprepared and unwilling. That can oftentimes be the difference between the adversity that brings out our better selves, and the tragedy that lays us low.

68. Valentina "Bullet" Shevchenko

"Not everything happens as we want or desire. It doesn't matter. I'm a fighter, and I'm ready to fight every time."

This is a perfect quote to encapsulate the ethos of 'stoicism'.

The power of the true stoic is to accept external problems, challenges, and difficulties with equanimity while at the same time tackling internal problems, challenges, and difficulties with tireless discipline.

The stoic does not seek any control over the outside world, and therefore is not bothered when the outside world does not behave as one wants. What the stoic seeks is internal discipline and peace. What makes stoicism work is the simple fact that we do indeed have much more control over ourselves and particularly over our own thoughts and feelings than we do over the outside world.

Valentina Shevchenko has had plenty of unexpected and difficult events in her life, but she's never complained about them or used them as excuses. In her very first fight for the UFC, she was brought in as a very late-notice replacement. Normally a fighter wants two to three months to prepare for any important match, but Shevchenko was ready to take her opportunity when it came, because, as a fighter, it's her job to be ready to fight every time.

She could not control when her opportunity would come and how much time she'd have to prepare for it, but she could control what kind of person she is, so that's what she did and what she still does.

69. Daniel "DC" Cormier

"Every day, I wake up, and I realise how lucky I am to be living this life."

Daniel Cormier is one of the few two-division champions of the UFC, having captured both the light heavyweight and heavyweight titles.

He also captured the XMMA, King of the Cage, and Strikeforce Grand Prix heavyweight championship belts before coming to the UFC, giving him the unusual distinction of being a world champion in every promotion he's ever fought for.

Aside from his multiple world championship pedigree, Cormier has also had a very successful run in his transition to UFC commentator and has continued to coach wrestling and MMA as well. All in all, Cormier is a man with a ton of talent and energy who has done an unimpeachable job of putting it to work for the sport.

This quote gives a hint at how Cormier has managed to be so successful for so long and in so many ways, as well as consistently make the right decisions, big and small, every day. It all begins with how you feel when you wake up. Cormier chooses to feel gratitude; gratitude for his talent, energy, health, and for the life those things have given him.

You may object that it's easy to feel gratitude when you're living a life like Cormier's. Well, that's undoubtedly true, but it's also true that Cormier wasn't born living this life. His father was killed when he was just seven years old. He had to work his way up the hard way in high school and college wrestling, and while he did make the Olympic team twice, he was forced to withdraw with kidney problems in 2008.

Cormier hasn't always had it easy, but his ability to be grateful for what he does have is one of the cornerstones of making the best of it.

70. Israel "The Last Stylebender" Adesanya

"You're never as good as they say you are. You're never as bad as they say you are. That's a quote I live by."

Israel makes a very insightful psychological point with this quote.

The way we see other people, especially celebrities, can easily become extreme. While we tend to have a very detailed understanding of our own lives, our view of the lives of other people is necessarily limited. We mostly see stars like MMA champions on their very best days and on their very worst days. We hear about their greatest accomplishments and their worst failings.

With this limited view of only the superlatives of their lives, we form superlative opinions very easily. With the rise of modern social media, we communicate and transmit those opinions very easily as well, and the more extreme the opinion, the more communicable and contagious it can become. This results in very extreme opinions becoming mainstream parts of the zeitgeist around celebrities, sports stars, politicians, or even social media personalities.

To a lesser degree, it affects everyone on social media as most social media platforms tend to emphasise the extreme in order to grab as much attention as possible.

Therefore, an understanding that you're never as far on the extreme, either good or bad, as people think you are, is the most healthy and balanced way to look at yourself. Even if you're not a celebrity, the people who do know of you but don't know you very well are judging you based on limited knowledge; it might be based on your best day or your worst day.

That doesn't make them bad–people have no choice but to judge others based on what little they do know– but it is healthy to bear in mind that people's judgements are inclined to leap towards extremes, especially when based on limited knowledge.

71. Urijah "The California Kid" Faber

"Dream big, stay positive, work hard and enjoy the journey."

These simple words of wisdom from the iconic WEC featherweight (145 lbs) champion and UFC hall-of-famer Urijah Faber demonstrate the mentality that has made him so successful for so long.

Faber dreamt big from a young age, graduating from the University of California-Davis with a bachelor's degree while at the same time competing at the NCAA level in wrestling.

He quickly went on to fight and win his first MMA matches in the Gladiator Challenge promotion in 2003. Pursuing an MMA career in 2003 (especially at bantamweight (135 lbs)) was a big dream, as MMA had not really yet begun to take off in North America at that time, and especially not in the lighter weight classes.

Urijah Faber's positivity was infectious, though. He didn't just ride the wave of increasing popularity of MMA in general and lighter weight class fights in particular–he was a very significant part of creating that wave. After becoming the WEC featherweight champion, his fan base grew continuously until the UFC was forced to take notice. A large part of the UFC purchase of the WEC and incorporating the lower weight classes that the WEC specialised in was thanks to the WEC stars that made it popular, and Urijah Faber's endearing positivity was a big part of his star power.

72. Anthony "Showtime" Pettis

"Attitude determines effort."

This short and sweet quote comes from a champion in one of the rarest of pantheons: a fighter with a move named for them.

Anthony "Showtime" Pettis will be forever immortalised for his famous "Showtime Kick", in which he leapt up, pushed off the cage with one foot, and landed an airborne roundhouse kick flush on the side of Benson Henderson's face, scoring a late fifth-round knockdown and securing an incredible decision victory for the final lightweight (155 lbs) championship fight of the WEC before its merger with the UFC. Pettis would rematch Henderson for the UFC lightweight title, which he would win by armbar, and though he lost the belt later on to Raphael Dos Anjos, he remained a perennial contender in three weight classes from featherweight (145 lbs) to welterweight (170 lbs).

This quote illustrates a simple psychological truth.

The amount of effort a person is capable of sustaining towards some goal is commensurate with their attitude about the value of achieving that goal and the importance of effort in doing so. Effort towards one thing represents the sacrifice of everything else, so it's critical that you have a positive attitude towards succeeding in that goal.

If you find yourself struggling to put in the effort needed to accomplish something, try taking a step back and examining your attitude towards that thing. Is it something you really value? Do you understand the importance of effort in achieving it? Taking some time to examine those questions and really nail down your attitude towards them can be a difficult but necessary step towards sustaining the right amount of effort to achieve what you really want in life.

73. Tito "The Huntington Beach Bad Boy" Ortiz

"Negativity just sucks the life out of somebody."

Tito Ortiz was one of the first and biggest MMA stars in the USA, becoming just the second man to become the UFC light heavyweight (205 lbs) champion and successfully defending the belt five straight times, a record for the division that held up for a decade.

It wasn't just his victories in the cage that made him a star, but also who he faced: fellow legends like Frank and Ken Shamrock, Chuck Lidell, Randy Couture, Wanderlei Silva and Vitor Belfort. Perhaps Tito Ortiz's most famous feud was with Ken Shamrock and his MMA team, "the Lion's Den", something which Dana White very cannily exploited by making Ortiz and Ken Shamrock rival coaches of season three of The Ultimate Fighter.

Ortiz's star power and career longevity, even in the face of a bad back injury that has required multiple surgeries, can only be attributed to his persistent positive thinking. He has always known his value and has never been afraid to go out and get it. His contract negotiations with Dana White were some of the most difficult White ever had to navigate, and Tito Ortiz never hesitated to try his hand at other ventures, including stints in professional wrestling and rival promotions like Affliction and Bellator, and even a farewell professional boxing match with Anderson Silva in 2021.

Most unusual and impressive of all, he even got himself elected Mayor pro tempore of his hometown of Huntington Beach in 2020. Clearly, Tito Ortiz has not allowed negativity to suck any life out of him.

74. Cat "Alpha" Zingano

"Life is going to present you with tons of problems. It's what you do about them that matters."

Cat Zingano is one of the great pioneers of women's MMA, and one of the toughest and most talented women ever to enter the Octagon.

In perhaps her most iconic performance, she came back from a first-round beating that left her dizzy and possibly concussed to win the bout with a third-round TKO against the legendary Amanda Nunes. Zingano was the last woman to ever beat the now seemingly untouchable UFC Champion.

However, Zingano has endured a lot more adversity than just that bout. Before that, an unlucky injury derailed her opportunity to coach TUF opposite mainstream star Ronda Rousey. Afterwards, Zingano struggled to fully recover from the Nunes match, and ended up dropping a string of decisions before finally snatching one back, only to then be forced out of a bout due to a freak eye injury from an errant kick that was ruled a TKO in favour of her opponent. Worst of all, Zingano was forced to become a single mother after the death of her husband in 2014.

She has not been presented with any shortage of problems by life, so she is speaking from firsthand experience with her quote. It's not the size of the problems that life presents us with that define us; it's how we deal with them.

Zingano has dealt with hers with true courage and tenacity, and that's what will forever define her.

75. Brandon "The Assassin Baby" Carrillo Moreno

"Maybe not today, and maybe not tomorrow or maybe not the next month, but one thing is true: I will be the champion one day. I promise!"

Brandon Carrillo Moreno is nothing if not a keeper of promises.

He made good on the promise in this quote by defeating Deiveson Figueiredo in a rematch in June of 2021 for the UFC flyweight (125 lbs) championship. Their first match ended in a heartbreaking majority draw, which meant Figueiredo, as the champion, kept his belt. After all, as the old saying in combat sports goes, "You have to beat the champ to be the champ". When Moreno finally won the championship, he became the first Mexican-born UFC champion.

Moreno kept working at his dream for a long time. He started training at 12, at first just to lose weight. His love and natural talent were ignited, though, and he ended up choosing an MMA career over his initial plans of studying law. His solid record and championship bona fides in the World Fighting Federation got him onto The Ultimate Fighter: Tournament of Champions, and from there, he was able to climb the ranks until finally seizing his chance with the rematch victory over Figueiredo.

His determination to stick to his dream until he accomplished it is a true testament to the power of positive thinking.

76. Holly "The Preacher's Daughter" Holm

"At the end of the day, you are in control of your own happiness. Life is going to happen whether you overthink it, overstress it, or not. Just experience life and be happy along the way. You can't control everything in your life, but you can control your happiness."

Holly Holm effectively preaches one of the core tenets of stoicism with this excellent quote.

The first key to being able to control your happiness is recognising that things are going to happen that you don't like or want or expect, no matter how much you overthink or 'overstress' about them. The second is learning to live in the moment, to experience things as they come, and to learn to savour that experience. Sometimes it will be a horrible experience that makes you feel awful, but the key to dealing with those moments is to live in them fully so that they pass by and through you more quickly. As you fully accept the negative sensations accompanying unpleasant and unwanted experiences, you may be able to come to the realisation that the source of the intensity of those negative sensations is their contrast to positive ones. Likewise, the source of intensity of whatever positive sensations you experience in good times is their contrast to negative ones.

When you can fully understand that, even in the moments of highest intensity, either good or bad, you can learn that happiness is under your control. Happiness is more than currently and constantly experiencing positive sensations–happiness is the ability to experience anything at all. Even negative sensations, like bad memories, pain, failure, regret, loss, all those sensations exist only in contrast to positive ones. They are just the other side of the coin of life. Once you can see that, you can choose to turn the coin over any time you like and see the positive on the other side.

It all starts with learning to experience life and being happy along the way, whatever else outside your control happens. Holly Holm has learned that power, and so can anyone with enough time and effort.

77. Alexander "The Mauler" Gustafsson

"Positive thinking is a habit. Like everything else, you get better at it with time."

Alexander Gustafsson is considered by some to be the best UFC fighter that hasn't won a title. He no doubt considers himself to be the best UFC fighter that hasn't won a title *yet*.

After coming up just short in three thrilling bouts for the UFC light heavyweight (205 lbs) championship, he's moved up to the UFC heavyweight (265 lbs) division. Gustafson has not battled his way into three title fights and then moved up a division to challenge the biggest men in the sport with a quitter's attitude or glum pessimism. On the contrary, he has worked hard all his life to cultivate the habit of positive thinking, and that is what has taken him so far.

There are many ways to build up the habit of positive thinking.

There is the practice of mindfulness: taking the time to really pay attention to your thoughts, and thereby take away their negative power. There is also the philosophy of 'stoicism': accepting that we cannot control what happens to us, but we can control ourselves and how we feel about and respond to what is happening around us.

Finally, there is the practice of gratitude: of purposefully recalling the good things in our life that we can be grateful for to counter negative thoughts of the unfairness of a seemingly cruel and unlucky existence. These habits of positive thinking can help us improve our lives from the inside out, and that's by far the most reliable and most sustainable way to do so.

As Alexander Gustafsson says, these habits of positive thinking are like anything else; the more we work on them, the easier and more effective it gets.

Chapter 5:

Mindset

A person's mindset consists of their beliefs about the world, themselves, and the relationship between them. It's a complex topic with many facets to explore.

There are many aspects to each person's mindset, and in this chapter, each quote from a world-class fighter will reveal an aspect of their mindset and how it helped them reach the greatness they achieved.

The beliefs that comprise your mindset form a crucial part of your character and personality and that, in turn, will have a lifelong influence on your success and happiness in life.

By reading about and understanding the mindsets of great MMA fighters, you can compare and contrast them with your own and begin the process of developing your mindset by choosing which parts of it are working well for you, and which parts you want to update.

That kind of introspection can be the next step on the road to the life you really want to live.

78. Brian "T-City" Ortega

"I'm dangerous because I have nothing to lose."

Brian Ortega's quote above demonstrates a core part of his mindset as a fighter.

The man with nothing to lose has nothing to fear from losing it. The man with nothing to fear is capable of doing much more.

Ortega's fighting style of constant aggression and going for finishes amply reflects this mindset. He is dangerous because he's willing to take the high-risk, high-reward chances whenever they come. He will commit when he gets an opening, and he will dive on submissions, especially guillotines and triangle chokes, whenever he gets the chance. Both the guillotine and the triangle choke are typically landed when in guard, a position which is normally seen as defensive and one a fighter should try to escape from.

Ortega is dangerous because he doesn't just defend and try to escape–he attacks from every position. That mindset has given him six submission wins by triangle choke or guillotine, and even when he doesn't get the tap, he has five more wins by decision, in no small part because judges prefer the aggressor and Ortega is always trying to be the aggressor.

The downside to this kind of mentality can be when you do have a lot to lose, and act recklessly rather than bravely. You have to take risks to get ahead in life, or to get anywhere at all, for that matter. In fact, in a manner of speaking, refusing to take any risks can be the biggest risk of all: it can lead to you getting stuck in a rut and missing out on all kinds of opportunities. Therefore, the best way to think about risk is to try to always take calculated risks, and to make sure that your calculations factor in the long-term risk of not taking any risks. However, real life doesn't always give you time to make careful calculations.

Adopting a "nothing to lose" mindset like Brian Ortega can be a great shortcut heuristic to make sure that you won't miss out on opportunities because of unnecessary hesitation or fear.

79. Frank Mir

"You know what the true definition of hell is? It's when you die; you get to meet the person you could have been."

Frank Mir is a true UFC legend. He holds many great distinctions, including the longest uninterrupted run as a UFC fighter: 16 years, from 2001 to 2016. He is also the first fighter to knock out the legendary Antônio Rodrigo "Minotauro" Nogueira, and the first fighter to submit him too.

Mir is also in that extremely exclusive club of fighters to have a move named after himself: an inside shoulder-lock from the guard that caught out and submitted Pete Williams, the only submission loss of his career. Mir is a two-time UFC heavyweight champion, winning his first belt by breaking the arm of then-champion Tim Sylvia, and his second by beating the Nogueira.

In between his heavyweight championship runs, Mir suffered a terrible motorcycle accident that snapped his femur in two places and destroyed all the ligaments of his knee. There was a good chance he'd never walk properly again, let alone fight. That is where the courage and determination of Mir were really proven. This brilliant quote shows a part of the mindset that got him through the toughest time of his life and back on the road to his second championship.

Hell is the worst place or the worst thing you can possibly imagine, and for Mir, that is regret at falling short compared to what he could have accomplished. Regret is possibly the most insidious of all emotions because it never really comes until it's already too late. Mir makes an excellent point that true hell is deathbed regrets because, at that point, there's literally nothing you can do about them. So, with that in mind, Mir lives his life to the absolute fullest.

The next time you feel like you lack the energy or motivation or even the courage to do something important, you know you should; imagine how you will feel about not doing it years from now, when you are old, dying, and completely unable to do much of anything.

That is what you should *really* fear.

80. Michael "The Count" Bisping

"I'm not going to please everyone; not everyone's going to like me. I accepted that a long time ago, and if I had to shed a tear every time I got a hate email, believe me, I'd be severely dehydrated."

A key aspect of mindset is learning how to think about how others think about you.

As social creatures, our social standing is extremely important to our wellbeing, so it's not as though we can afford to go through life making enemies or being totally uncaring of whatever anyone else thinks about us. However, we must not err too far in the other direction either.

Michael Bisping's quote shows us his winning mindset on how to understand our social obligations and status. As he says, not everyone is going to like him, or anyone for that matter. He's made his peace with that, and at some point, so must everyone else.

Sometimes you have to make hard choices that will please some people and annoy others. Trying to please everybody all of the time is not only impossible, but it's also counter-productive at a certain point. Humans have very finely tuned senses for authenticity—and for its opposite. Since we all know it's impossible to please everybody all of the time, any efforts to do so are usually seen through sooner or later as inauthentic and deceptive, even manipulative, and so ultimately are counterproductive. Furthermore, if you cannot accept that not everyone is going to like you, you'll end up devastated by everyone who doesn't.

Bisping's mindset threads the needle effectively.

It's not as though he doesn't care about what *anyone* thinks of him. He just understands and accepts that not *everyone* is going to like him. Nobody can be all things to all people. What you can be is the best person you can be, for yourself, and for the people you care about most. If you're doing your best, then you won't have to worry too much about what everyone else thinks of you. Those who know you well will respect you, and while there will always be those who don't, that's okay. That's life.

81. Cris "Cyborg" Venancio

"Love me or hate me, it's all in my favour. If you love me, I'll always be in your heart. If you hate me, I'll always be in your mind."

"Cyborg" shows the perfect mindset for a fighter and an entertainer with this quote.

For a 'normal' person, sure, it's probably better if as few people as possible hate you. Most people would be perfectly happy to go through life without anyone hating them, if at all possible. For a prizefighter, though, being hated might be as good as being loved. "Cyborg" understands that perfectly. The difference when you're a prizefighter, is explained in her quote. For a normal person, someone who hates you, an enemy, is capable of causing you harm. That's normally something you'd want to avoid.

However, for a prizefighter like "Cyborg", if fans love her, great: they'll tune in to watch her win. If fans hate her, that works too: they'll tune in to watch her fight, hoping she gets beat. And if an opponent hates her: that's also great. That means she'll always be in their mind, distracting them, antagonising them, encouraging them to fight more recklessly, and she'll meet their aggression with her own implacable abilities. Her string of TKO and KO victories attests to the fact that there's nothing that plays into her game more than a wildly aggressive opponent willing to trade punches.

What does this quote tell us about how a 'normal' person should craft their mindset?

Perhaps, that there is no such thing as a 'normal' person, and everyone should craft their mindset according to their own unique circumstances and values. That's what "Cyborg" has done, and it's worked out brilliantly.

82. Royce Gracie

"I take all the opportunities that come my way, and I am thankful that I have them."

Royce Gracie proved the truth of this quote beyond all shadow of a doubt when he accepted the opportunity to represent his family and his art in the first UFC.

Just try to put yourself in his shoes in 1993. He had not competed in any professional bouts before. The profession barely existed outside of some show-matches and rather shady no-holds-barred fighting rings. The UFC was the Gracie family's first big attempt to bring their unique and uniquely effective style of martial arts to the mainstream–to prove once and for all that their way of fighting was the most practical and effective for everyone.

All that pressure fell to Royce Gracie.

Imagine how scary it must have been to be expected, with no real professional experience, giving up a big size disadvantage to nearly all your highly trained, dangerous, and confident opponents, to go out and represent the honour and skill of your family in a winner-take-all single-elimination one-day tournament.

He had to go out and defeat three opponents, one after the other, on the same day, to accomplish his mission. Royce's mindset was positively amazing if you really think about it. He didn't resent the responsibility put on him and the obvious danger he was being asked to put himself in. Instead, he viewed it as a great opportunity, and he was thankful to have it. Then, he went out and accomplished his mission, and despite how scared anyone would have been in his shoes, he did it calmly and made it look easy.

That's why he will go down in history as one of the greatest of all pioneers in this sport. It makes you ask yourself: what opportunity will you be thankful to take on?

83. Cat "Alpha" Zingano

"Nothing always stays the same. You don't stay happy forever. You don't stay sad forever."

Cat Zingano's quote echoes a key concept in psychology known as the 'hedonic treadmill' or 'hedonic adaptation'.

What it means is that psychologically we tend to adapt to even the biggest events in our life so that their psychological impacts on our happiness or sadness naturally wear off over time. The best day of your life makes you very happy for a while, but as time goes by, you get used to whatever it was that made that day so great and return to your normal baseline level of happiness. The same goes for even the worst day of your life: whatever terrible event happened, you gradually get used to the fact that it happened, that your life is whatever it is now, and the negative emotions associated with it gradually fade to the background as you return to your normal baseline. Of course, some medical conditions like depression or addiction can interfere with this process, but those aside, what Cat Zingano said is basically true. Whatever happiness or sadness you're feeling in the moment will fade into the past as time goes by.

What does this mindset imply about how we should live our lives?

It shows that however intensely we are feeling in the moment, that intensity will not last. So, if we are intensely happy about something, we should savour it as best we can; try to enjoy every detail and fix it in our memory. Likewise, whenever a bad thing happens that makes us miserable, we can also take a moment to realise that that misery too is temporary and will fade. That doesn't mean we should just ignore it, of course; the point of negative emotions is to motivate us to fix or learn to avoid whatever is making us miserable.

Once we have done that, however, our negative emotions have served their useful purpose, and we can let them go with a clear conscience.

84. Rafael Dos Anjos

"Everybody likes money. I like money. I need money to survive. But I don't love money. Money is not my god."

How we think about money, and the role it plays in our lives, is a critical aspect of our mindset. It is easy to oversimplify such a complex topic, and nearly everybody has an emotional bias of some sort regarding money because of how important it is.

The challenge is to overcome whatever emotional biases we have and try to look at money and our relationship to it as objectively as possible. Rafael Dos Anjos, former UFC lightweight (155 lbs) champion, shows that he has done just that with this wise quote. He acknowledges the utility of money but refuses a higher emotional connection to it or need for it.

At the end of the day, money represents two things: what people are willing to give you in exchange for your time and effort and talent, and what you have available to give other people for theirs. It's easy to see the emotional component there: it reflects not just on your survival but also on your ego, as it puts a number on your economic value to others.

However, money is a very imperfect and incomplete measure of a person's true moral value and dignity. It's far more psychologically healthy to view money as nothing more than what it is: a convenient medium by which you can exchange useful things with others.

Placing undue emotional and psychological value on money gives it more power over you than is useful.

85. Miesha "Cupcake" Tate

"I hate the stereotype that women who fight are 'butch' or 'wannabe men'. It's nice to be able to embrace being a beautiful, strong woman."

Miesha Tate's quote above shows how she forms her own mindset by rejecting the stereotypes of others. She has certainly lived up to the words of her quote and more, after winning both a Strikeforce and UFC championship belt.

Her quote speaks to more than just physical beauty and strength as well. There are few things more beautiful and strong than being true to yourself and following your own dreams, even in the face of scepticism or negative stereotyping.

The tendency to stereotype can sometimes be a useful or at least unavoidable heuristic shortcut, but it is always better by far to try to form opinions of people as unique and complex individuals rather than as just a simple stereotypical avatar of some set of identity markers. By the same token, people can all too easily allow themselves to be pigeonholed by stereotypical expectations put on them by others.

If you happen to already fit nicely into standard, accepted and traditional expectations, that's great, but if not, you have every right to examine those expectations and come to your own conclusions about them. If you do so honestly and in good faith, you will almost always find a way, like Miesha Tate has, to best express yourself according to your own values, desires, and talents, while still finding a way to fit into your community and society as a whole.

86. Anderson "The Spider" Silva

"You must have a dragon inside you. When you need, you let the dragon out."

Anderson Silva's quote above reflects a Jungian view of human psychology, something which Carl Jung referred to as 'integrating the shadow'.

The basic idea is that our personalities are composed of two parts. There is an outward, socially acceptable part, called the 'persona', which we show to other people because it is polite, agreeable, cooperative, and pleasant.

As children, during the process of socialisation, we are taught what other people like to see in us, and we learn through positive and negative reinforcement to show those traits as much as we can. But, there is another part of us we keep hidden below the persona: that part Jung called the 'shadow'.

The shadow is there to protect us; it is our anger, our jealousy, our envy, our suspicion, aspects of our personality that are disagreeable and unpleasant to others, but necessary for our survival under extreme circumstances when we are genuinely threatened or abused by someone who intends to do us harm.

Jung believed that most people simply try to repress their shadow. He believed that the pleasant mask of the persona was something that could not only hide our shadow from others and stifle it, but from ourselves as well. But when we do that, ultimately, only one of two things can happen: either our shadow will burst out uncontrollably and quite possibly inappropriately at the wrong times, causing harm to ourselves and others unnecessarily; or we will successfully squash our shadow down to the point that we become utterly incapable of protecting ourselves even when appropriate, and turn ourselves into victims to every unscrupulous person that bumps into us.

Integrating the shadow means confronting it, accepting it, and learning to use your shadow to defend yourself when appropriate and quiet it when it's not needed. That is what Anderson Silva's quote is all about: you must turn your shadow into a dragon you can unleash when it's needed, and control when it's not.

And that is what training in martial arts is really all about.

87. Daniel "DC" Cormier

"No matter how bad things get, eventually, the sun is going to shine. If you just keep at it, pursuing your goals, eventually, good things happen to decent people. For a person who is set on his goals, good things will happen. Everyone deals with adversity. It's how you bounce back from it."

Daniel Cormier's quote reflects a mindset of fundamental optimism and faith in the justice of the world.

Some people would consider this kind of optimism and faith as blind and foolish naivety about the true indifference or even banal cruelty of the universe towards fragile little mortals like us. The problem with that viewpoint is the same as the advantage of Cormier's: our mindset is often the first step in generating a self-fulfilling prophecy. Of course, there are no guarantees in life–random, senseless tragedy can strike anyone at any time for any reason. But there are probabilities and likelihoods. Even though you can't guarantee that tragedy won't strike you down, having the best mindset gives you the best odds of success.

By the same token, having a negative, pessimistic, cynical, or even nihilistic viewpoint will contribute to negative, pessimistic, cynical, and even nihilistic behaviours, and that will only make having any kind of long-term successful and happy life much more unlikely.

When you think negatively, you are more likely to act negatively, to lash out in anger or frustration or to give up at the first sign of real adversity. And then, when the consequences of your rash negative actions or quitting hit you, your first instinct is to blame the harsh and unjust world, which only reinforces your negative mindset and creates more negative behaviour in a vicious cycle.

If instead you take to heart Cormier's quote, and you bounce back from adversity, stick to your goals, and believe in a fundamentally fair world where eventually good things happen to decent people who stay positive, then that mindset will generate behaviours that are more likely to make that positive outcome happen. There are no guarantees in life, but why not give yourself the best odds? Doing so is going to make you happier, even in the short run anyway.

As far as naivety goes, wouldn't it be a sight to see someone with the guts to call six-time world champion Daniel Cormier 'naive' to his face? There's not a naive bone left in DC's body, and reflexive pessimism and cynicism certainly isn't any wiser than naivety in any case.

88. Israel "The Last Stylebender" Adesanya

"All that matters is how you see yourself."

As evidenced by this quote, Israel Adesanya's view on self-image is that it is more important than anyone else's image of you.

There are a few good reasons for this. The first is that nobody else has to live with you—only you do. The second is that nobody else can see inside your own heart and mind, and nobody else can see everything you do every day—only you can. The third is that nobody else can hold you accountable better than you can hold yourself. Finally, worrying about anyone else's view of you more than your own isn't very productive or helpful.

At the end of the day, if you are honest with yourself and search your own conscience in good faith, you know what you want to do and who you want to be and whether you are on the right path or not. And if you aren't; if you are in the habit of self-deception, self-aggrandisement, or self-flagellation, it doesn't really matter what anyone else thinks of you either, because you can deceive other people, or shut them out of your life, if necessary, even more easily than you already shut your own conscience out.

That's why it really only matters how you see yourself. If you see yourself honestly, and you set yourself on the path you want to be on, true to your values and aligned with your talents and desires, then you'll act in such a way as to earn the respect of others without ever having to worry much about how they see you anyway.

89. Mark Hunt

"None of us is promised tomorrow...so, whenever an opportunity has presented itself, I'm willing to take it."

Mark Hunt, the king of the walk-off KO (where the winning fighter walks away from a knocked-out opponent before the referee even needs to step in to stop it), is one of the all-time great fighters and characters of the MMA world. The mindset he expresses with this quote was proven for him at a very young age.

Born in a big family, Hunt was a troubled child growing up and ended up in jail twice for violent offences. Shortly after getting out of jail for the second time, he got into an altercation in front of a nightclub in which he knocked out several other men. A bouncer at the club witnessed the incident and, impressed with Hunt's apparent latent talent for violence, invited him to come train at his Muay Thai club. Within a week, Hunt had scored his first Muay Thai victory.

Mark Hunt rocketed up the ranks in kickboxing, never turning down a fight and winning most of them even when he was 'supposed' to be just a steppingstone to other up-and-coming fighters. He ended up getting invited to the premier kickboxing tournament of the time, K-1, and was the first to compete in the Oceania regional qualifying tournament. Despite being a heavy underdog, as usual, Mark Hunt accepted the opportunity and won the tournament with three straight victories. He went on to have a very successful if relatively brief career in K-1, winning the premier title, the K-1 World Grand Prix, in just his second try. Never one to turn down an opportunity, Hunt then accepted opportunities to fight in MMA for Pride, Dream, and the UFC, where he was a perennial contender and fan favourite for well over a decade.

The mindset of being willing to just say 'yes' can take you surprisingly far, and Hunt is living proof of that.

90. Kamaru Usman

"You never say never. That's one of the lessons I've learned."

Kamaru Usman is one of the most dominant champions in the UFC today.

His winning streak, including six title defences, sits at 19, the record for the UFC welterweight (170 lbs) division, which was once held by the legendary Georges St. Pierre. If Usman keeps up this dominant streak much longer, he may be regarded as surpassing even GSP's legendary run at welterweight.

Usman's mindset of never saying never has a lot of applications.

Firstly, it's good advice to never count anyone out, especially yourself. He exemplified that himself by going from missing the Olympics due to injuries and failure to making the team to launching himself into one of the all-time great MMA careers.

Secondly, it's good advice to avoid using the word 'never' (or its opposite, 'always') when arguing with anyone, including yourself. Using such hyperbolic language in an emotionally difficult time is almost always counter-productive.

Finally, if you avoid thinking or speaking in absolutes, you'll avoid looking and feeling silly when they inevitably prove untrue.

91. Rickson Gracie

"I always keep my mind open. For me, a mind has to work like a parachute, works only if it's open."

The wonderful imagery of the metaphor in this quote really makes it stick.

The idea of a mind as a parachute is lovely on many levels. As we know, a parachute only works when it's open. And what does it do when it's open? It spreads out to catch the air, slowing you down to protect you, so you gently come down to earth. A well-functioning mind does the same: it protects you by being open to any good ideas that can help you avoid calamity when you're in danger. A closed mind, like a packed parachute, catches nothing. Then, when danger comes, you crash headlong right into it.

Much like a parachute, a mind has to be more than just open all the time, though. It must be neatly and carefully packed; this is akin to the kind of training and discipline that martial arts–or any good, long-term dedication towards learning a useful skill or attaining a higher education–can give you.

Your mind must also be deployed at the right time. Opening your parachute while you're still in the plane doesn't help you any, nor does opening it when you're already too close to the ground. You must be able to recognise when it's most important to open your mind, when you're in need of new ideas to get you out of a bad situation or just a rut. You can't walk around with your mind open constantly, any more than even an experienced skydiver drags around an open parachute with him everywhere he goes.

But, you have to keep it ready to open when needed, and that's where discipline and training cannot be taken for granted.

92. Khabib "The Eagle" Nurmagomedov

"When you have a hard life, a tough life, success becomes very easy."

.

The logic of this quote may seem a little tough to follow at first, but when you see all the unsaid steps, it makes perfect sense.

Khabib Nurmagomedov is talking about what kind of person a hard, tough life can create. Some people can be made bitter or fearful by a hard life, but others can choose to learn and grow from their difficult circumstances into stronger, wiser people. For those people, success can and does come relatively easier. The key question is, what separates the second type of people from the first? How is it that some people get wiser and stronger from a hard life, while others just remain cynical or hopeless?

Khabib's life gives us some clues.

He was undoubtedly raised in a very tough place. Born in the Republic of Dagestan in Russia, he was surrounded by both poverty and political and religious turmoil. What made his life different from many of his peers was his father, a decorated veteran and an expert in judo and sambo and a youth wrestling coach. He was determined to offer the youth of his village an alternative to Islamic extremism through wrestling, and he brought Khabib up with martial arts. Khabib's life was anything but easy, both in terms of his community environment and in terms of his training, starting wrestling seriously at just eight years old, but it was exactly the kind of hard, tough life that can breed a champion.

Khabib listed his four inspirations as first his father, but also Muhammad Ali, Mike Tyson, and footballer Ronaldo. So, the real answer is not pointless, random suffering and tragedy: it's discipline, training, and a measured exposure to both the negative and the positive possibilities of life that can make success come more easily.

93. Fabricio "Vai Cavalo" Werdum

"You're not poor because you don't have money. You're poor if you don't have a dream."

This is a beautiful quote from one of the great inspiring champions of MMA.

Fabricio Werdum was a top-level Brazilian Jiu-Jitsu competitor for years before getting his big break in MMA. That really came when he was brought on as a training partner for the legendary Mirko "Cro-Cop" Filipovic. He was able to leverage that opportunity into a shot at heavyweight fighting in Pride FC. He was immediately recognised as a serious threat because of his jiu-jitsu skills, but widely considered too one-dimensional to ever win a major championship.

When matched with top-level superior strikers or well-rounded fighters like Sergei Kharitonov, Antonio Rodrigo Nogueira or Andrei Arlovski, he often lost by decision after struggling to get into a position to score a submission win, though he did also score very notable victories over great fighters like Alistair Overeem, Alexander Emelianenko and Gabriel Gonzaga.

He seemed destined to be considered one of the all-time great gatekeepers. He was the guy you have to get past to be champion but was unlikely to ever be champion himself.

That all changed in 2010.

He found himself in Strikeforce across the cage from the Last Emperor, the unbeatable Fedor Emelianenko himself. Werdum then promptly shocked the world by finishing a triangle choke and handing Fedor the first real defeat of his life. Suddenly everyone had to wake up to the fact that Werdum was not just a gatekeeper. If he could submit Fedor, he could submit anyone. The point was proven in 2015, when Werdum finally clinched the premier heavyweight title, the UFC heavyweight championship, after beating Mark Hunt to claim the interim belt and Cain Velasquez to make it undisputed.

Werdum's quote, like his biography, speaks for itself.

An amount of money is just a number; true poverty is the lack of a dream. Likewise, true wealth is having that dream and working towards it, every day. If you have a dream that you can work on, you're not truly poor. It's when you don't have one that you are.

94. Dan "Hendo" Henderson

"I don't believe in superstition. It's bad luck."

Dan Henderson is one of those rare legends who came into the sport as a true pioneer and remained a serious championship contender for his entire 19-year professional career.

His first fights were in 1997, when he easily won a one-night four-man tournament in Brazil with two quick victories. His last fight was for the UFC middleweight (185 lbs) championship against an old rival, Michael Bisping, in 2016. He was 46 years old.

What has made Henderson such an incredibly enduring and effective fighter in MMA? Many fans and analysts would point to his well-rounded style: excellent Greco-Roman wrestling combined with a devastating overhand right means his opponents never know what to defend.

Many would also point to his excellent conditioning and durability, something he showcased in his multiple extended wars with fellow middleweight and light heavyweight (205 lbs) legend Wanderlei Silva. Still, others would talk about his flexibility and adaptability over time: he always had a game plan for every opponent and always had a way to win, even against larger and seemingly more dangerous fighters like Fedor Emelianenko.

What would Henderson himself say? Well, as this quote might hint, whatever he'd say, he'd probably say it with his typical wry wit. Maybe he'd just call himself lucky; after all, since he doesn't believe in superstition, he hasn't suffered from the bad luck it brings. Clearly, 19 years of success, championships and incredible upsets aren't all luck. Having a sense of humour undoubtedly helps a lot too. That aside, as usual, there's some truth beneath the humour.

The psychological root of superstitions is to try to gain some sense of control over the uncontrollable, like luck. The problem comes when we fully believe in our superstitions and receive from them some kind of sign that bad luck is coming our way. This creates a self-fulfilling prophecy where believing that bad luck is coming makes us perform worse, and then we really do fail.

The best way to avoid such a possibility is to just follow Dan Henderson's advice: if you don't believe in superstitions, they won't give you any bad luck!

95. Alistair "The Demolition Man" Overeem

"Fighting is life….Are you a person who gives up, or are you a person who's going to fight?"

Alistair Overeem eloquently sums up a champion's mindset with this quote.

Fighting is life, and life is fighting. This isn't only true of fighters. Even for people who never get into a physical fight, metaphorical fighting is something we all do every day. We sometimes fight with others, we sometimes fight with our environment or difficult circumstances, but most of all, we all fight with ourselves.

Our better natures are always in conflict with our short-term desires and immediate negative emotions. Every day is a new battle between what we know, deep down, is right for us in the long-run, and what will make us feel a little better right now. What kind of person you are is in large part determined by whether your better nature wins out more often, or whether it just gives up and lets you do what feels good right now.

Alistair Overeem is a fighter in the least abstract meaning of the term. He has fought and won championships all over the world for two decades. He isn't just talking about himself, though; metaphorically, we are all fighters, fighting our own battles. He won his championship fights not just by defeating his opponents, but by first defeating his own fears, laziness, and anything else inside himself that was standing in his own way.

We must all fight and win those same battles, and if we do, then we can get down to making our own dreams come true, whatever they may be.

96. Chael Sonnen

"I have never asked the crowd for their approval, and I will never start."

Chael Sonnen's mindset towards the crowd is aptly summarised in this short quote: He isn't out for their approval, and he never will be.

What does he really mean by this, though?

Firstly, you have to understand what he means by 'the crowd'. He isn't talking about the most important people in his life: his family, his friends, his colleagues and his bosses. He's talking about bystanders who are only witnessing his exploits from a certain distance and a certain perspective.

As a prizefighter, he doesn't need any of them to approve of him; he just needs them to watch. Wishing for their approval is therefore not only unneeded, but it may also be counter-productive for his purposes. After all, how much attention can you really get by merely being 'approved of'?

Chael Sonnen made himself a major PPV draw and fan favourite not by being approved of, but by being controversial, exciting, outrageous, by turns endearing and infuriating. He famously antagonised basically the entire country of Brazil in the build-up to his match with beloved Brazilian star Wanderlei Silva. Millions of

Brazilians disapproved of him very strongly—so they tuned in to watch their hometown hero fight him. And that was just fine by Sonnen. Now his podcast and other media appearances continue to have a huge fan base while he brutally honestly, even almost cheerfully, admits to controversial past actions like using PEDs. Do people approve of such things? No, but it certainly gets attention.

Ultimately, what we can all learn from Chael here is not what is specifically relevant only to him as a prizefighter and entertainer, but rather that it's worth looking objectively at what is really important in your life. Chael realised immediately that the crowd's approval was not objectively important at all to his career as a prizefighter and entertainer; only their attention was. That realisation freed him up to act far more intelligently in his best interests than if he had been eager for the crowd's approval. We can all stand to similarly take a look at what we are working towards in our life that, actually, isn't objectively important at all.

If we can find things we are chasing that we really don't actually need, we can, like Chael Sonnen, free ourselves up to concentrate on what's really important.

97. Donald "Cowboy" Cerrone

"Just do whatever you want to in life. One day tomorrow won't be there."

Donald "Cowboy" Cerrone is one of those rare fighters whose nickname has become far more well-known than their real name.

"Cowboy" is as apt as it is obvious: Cerrone, after all, is a man who rode bulls before he even took up MMA. Cerrone is also one of those fighters who appear to be in it mainly for a love of fighting.

He has 54 MMA fights and 29 kickboxing fights, along with a single professional boxing match. Although he has contended for the UFC title once and had a few shots at the WEC title before it merged with the UFC, he has never won and has not really been in serious contention for years. Yet he goes out and fights very frequently for a top-level fighter, and regularly wins the Performance of the Night or Fight of the Night honours.

Cerrone appears to be a man who just likes to fight and is simply living according to the mindset he expressed in this quote.

Is this wise advice for everyone, though? Doesn't just doing whatever you want in life ultimately lead to trouble?

Of course, it depends on what you really want.

If what you really want is to just immediately satisfy whatever impulse comes over you moment to moment, that's probably not going to work out too well for you in the long run. However, if you take the time to carefully examine what you really want in the overall run of your entire life and then work towards that wisely and diligently, it should work out for you very well.

What Cerrone's mindset is really about is avoiding regrets from missed opportunities and unpursued dreams. That's something we can all learn from.

98. Tony "El Cucuy" Ferguson

"I never make the same mistake twice. If you catch me slipping one time, good for you, but it ain't gonna happen again."

Tony Ferguson's mindset towards mistakes is what you'd expect from a great MMA fighter like him, and one we can all try to emulate.

Everyone is going to make mistakes in life; in fact, we often make so many that we don't even notice them all—just the ones that life, or a canny opponent, can punish us for. What's most important, though, is that we learn from our mistakes and try not to make them again. What's most difficult is learning the right lessons from our mistakes. This is where so many people really go wrong.

When something bad happens, it's easy to see that a mistake has been made. It's harder on our ego, but still easy enough to see when it's our own mistake, and that we ourselves need to change something to avoid making it again. What's hardest of all is knowing precisely what it is that we need to change to correct the mistake.

When we're dealing with complex problems, and real-life problems are usually complex, it's a lot easier to see what's gone wrong than it is to figure out how to make it go right. Sometimes the only solution is trial and error. That takes courage, persistence and determination, but sometimes that's the best you've got.

It's better by far to keep failing in different ways until something works than it is to keep failing in the same way, or to fail permanently by giving up altogether.

99. "Thug" Rose Namajunas

"I'm like a tree. My leaves might change colour, but my roots are the same."

The poetic imagery in this quote points to a deeper truth about the difference between values and goals or desires.

The leaves of a tree change colour or even fall off in winter, in much the same way as a person's desires and goals are adapted to their specific environment and circumstances. The roots of the tree that are stable, and hidden from plain sight, are a person's true values. Your values are what everything else must grow out of, and they are what will remain the most stable throughout your life.

What this implies about our mindset is that our mindset should always begin with a careful examination and understanding of our roots: our true, core values. Since that's what everything else in our mindset is going to grow out of, for our mindset to be sustainable and healthy in the long run, it has to be based on our core values.

It also implies that people's true values are not always in plain sight. You can judge a tree by its leaves, but not that accurately. You need to go deeper, look beneath the surface, to really understand someone. Their leaves will change with the seasons, as they should; it's their roots that show who they really are.

Chapter 6:

Focus

The ability to focus on one thing is essential in maximising both the efficiency and quality of your output in any field.

For a brief time in recent history, 'multitasking' was all the rage. Still, economists and psychologists that took the time to study the phenomenon quickly realised what has become known as 'the myth of multitasking'. In reality, people can only focus on one thing at a time and attempting to 'multitask' really means rapidly switching your focus from one thing to another.

The problem with this habit is that it takes a certain amount of time to get focused and efficiently work on a given problem or task; the more often you switch your focus, the more time is wasted on just refocusing.

In the modern world filled with the distractions of screens and social media feeds constantly battling for our attention, staying focused on a single thing for any length of time feels more demanding than ever. That rarity makes it more valuable for those who can do it.

MMA fighters have learned to deal with distractions and stay focused the hard way.

If you start thinking about the latest celebrity gossip or what your friends will think of your new cat or what movie you might want to catch on the weekend, or what TV series you want to catch up on while you're sparring or rolling in an MMA club, you'll soon find yourself brought back to the moment by a solid punch you missed or by getting submitted. If you want to work on your focus without using physical pain as a motivator, mindfulness meditation and yoga are a couple of great ways to get started.

In this chapter, quotes on the value and wisdom of focus from fighters who have mastered it should help give you all the motivation and inspiration needed to get started on working on maximising your own ability to focus.

100. Dominick "The Dominator" Cruz

"I'm ready to live in the present—not in the past and not in the future—because in the present is where there's peace."

A key part of developing focus is learning to let go of dwelling or ruminating on the past and to avoid worrying about or anticipating the future.

Thinking too much about negative past events can distract you with regrets and fill you with too much fear of repeating mistakes, making you hesitant and unconfident. By the same token, thinking too fondly of the past can make you overly nostalgic and detract from your ability to appreciate and enjoy the good things happening now. Learning the lessons of the past, good and bad, is necessary for progress and growth, but once you have learned those lessons, you also have to learn to let go of their emotional impact on you.

Similarly, fearing the future and focusing on possible negative outcomes can give you 'target fixation' and only make the negative outcomes more likely to happen in a self-fulfilling prophecy. On the other hand, looking forward too much to some utopian future can also rob you of your ability to enjoy what you have today, and, in extreme circumstances, it can even be used to justify negative actions to achieve hypothetically positive outcomes. "The ends justify the means" can often be a dangerous rationalisation that can result in good people doing bad things. It's good to live your life in such a way that your future will be benefited as a result of your present actions but living in the future too much also has its clear drawbacks.

As Dominick Cruz says, only by living in the present can you find peace. Focus on what you're doing, feeling, and thinking right here and right now, as much as you can. That is the best way by far to avoid the pitfalls of living too much in the past or the future.

101. Donald "Cowboy" Cerrone

"I tend to worry about now, now, and I'll worry about then, then."

Donald Cerrone will probably never be accused of failing to live in the now.

Few people are more dedicated to squeezing every last drop of life out of every moment than "Cowboy". While he may sometimes be accused of insufficiently caring about the possible future consequences of his actions, this quote is typical of his thinking on such criticisms. It's actually a fairly cogent quote on the utility of focus.

Of course, one shouldn't act as if the future doesn't matter or will never exist. You should always try to be at least mentally prepared for some likely future scenarios, if nothing else; otherwise, it's like you're walking around with your eyes closed, bumping into everything at random and getting surprised by it every time.

What "Cowboy" refuses to do is to get stuck in 'analysis paralysis', calculating endless hypotheticals and spending valuable time preparing for things that may or may not ever happen. His philosophy is that by far, the worst possible future outcome is a future filled with regrets about opportunities not taken or enjoyed in the present.

By focusing on the present, you not only enjoy the present, but you also put yourself in the best position to avoid living a life of regret in the future.

102. BJ Penn

"Birds fly and fish swim, and I do this."

BJ Penn, legendary UFC lightweight (155 lbs) champion and considered for a time to be the greatest lightweight fighter ever, is a man who doesn't just love to compete; he loves to fight.

By 'this' in his quote, he means fighting. There are those who may consider his legacy somewhat tarnished by his poorer performances when he continued to fight late in his career and well past his prime, but BJ Penn is a man who clearly could not have done otherwise. He spent his whole life focused on fighting, and he couldn't just walk away from it in his prime. He had to go on for as long as his body would physically let him. That's what made him so great in the first place.

Much like the Zen Buddhist saying of 'chop wood, carry water', what BJ Penn did before he was 'enlightened', before he was champion, was train to fight and fight–and what BJ Penn did after he was champion was train to fight and fight.

BJ Penn got his start in martial arts by achieving a Brazilian Jiu-Jitsu black belt in just three years of training—something which skilled athletes training regularly take at least ten years to achieve. Silencing any sceptics on whether he deserved the black belt so early, within weeks of earning his black belt, BJ Penn competed in the World Jiu-Jitsu Championships in Rio De Janeiro and became the first non-Brazilian to win in the black belt division. He then went on to become a multi-division champion in the UFC, winning both the lightweight and welterweight (170 lbs) belts, a K-1 champion, and, as Dana White put it, the first crossover pay-per-view star of lower weight divisions and the man who built the 155 lbs division for the UFC.

You can't rack up a list of accomplishments like that before you're even 30 years old without some incredible focus.

103. Justin "The Highlight" Gaethje

"I'll worry about things I can control."

World Series of Fighting and one-time UFC interim lightweight (155 lbs) champion Justin Gaethje elucidates a critical aspect of focus with this quote.

A necessary component of the ability to focus is knowing what to focus on, and Gaethje hits the nail on the head by focusing on what he can control. Much like the past and the future can be distractions from the present, the actions of other people or the environment or just bad luck are also things that can pointlessly distract us. By focusing only on what you yourself can personally control–most importantly your own thoughts and actions–you concentrate your energy and attention in the most efficient possible way.

Worrying about others or about bad luck just takes time and energy away from what you can personally change and affect. As the great stoic Epictetus put it, "There is one path to happiness, and that is to cease worrying about things which are beyond the power of our will". Worry about what you can control and accept the things which you cannot.

Justin Gaethje came up just short in his UFC title opportunity against Khabib Nurmagomedov, but then again, so did literally everyone else. Justin refocused on what he could control–his own training and performance–and he put up a stellar fight to bounce back and defeat former Bellator champion Michael Chandler. That Fight of the Night performance makes a strong argument for him to gain another title shot, but what Gaethje is focused on is himself. That's what will give him the best chance to win an undisputed championship in the UFC, so that's what he's doing.

104. Joanna Jędrzejczyk

"I don't do fights on Twitter."

Joanna Jędrzejczyk, as usual, manages to be both wise and menacing in this quote.

The menacing part is the implied threat: she doesn't "do fights on Twitter" because she does them in real-life. The wise part is the admonition to avoid pointless social media quarrels altogether. This is another excellent point about where and what to focus your attention on.

Social media platforms like Twitter, Facebook and many others, make their money off of 'engagement': the more people they have spending time on their platform, the more money they can sell advertising space for. Their algorithms designed to maximise 'engagement' quickly, if unconsciously, discovered that the best way to get engagement is to get people angry and scared. Angry and scared people spend more time on the platform, angrily reading and arguing with each other, and as a result, advertisements meant to reach them become more valuable and more profitable.

Joanna Jędrzejczyk avoids falling into that trap, and so should everyone. There's absolutely nothing to be gained by anyone apart from advertising sales teams and executives by fighting on Twitter.

Focus on what makes you better, happier, and more successful, not on what makes more money for someone else hoping to profit off your anger.

105. Lyoto "The Dragon" Machida

"You need to have goals in life. My father always says that when you have no goals in life, you have no reason to live."

Lyoto Machida was not the first or the only fighter to come into the UFC with a karate background, but he undoubtedly did more than anyone to restore its credibility in the West as a legitimate martial art after grapplers like wrestlers and Brazilian Jiu-Jitsu practitioners had dominated the sport for so long and even the successful strikers in the sport almost all had Muay Thai or kickboxing backgrounds.

Machida's unique and clearly karate-based style was greeted with a lot of scepticism when he came into the UFC in 2007, despite his 8-0 professional record in Brazil and Japan. He quickly won over the critics and sceptics with another eight straight wins in the UFC, culminating in winning the UFC light heavyweight (205 lbs) championship from wrestler Rashad Evans and then defending the belt against Muay Thai and Brazilian Jiu-Jitsu expert Mauricio "Shogun" Rua.

Machida learned his skills and his discipline mainly from his father, Shotokan karate master Yoshizo Machida. Goals are necessary for a successful and fulfilling life. To a master like Yoshizo, goals are necessary to live.

The ability to focus on your goals is also essential. Every day that you are not focused on accomplishing your own goals, you are living your life for something or someone else. Be very careful where you spend your time and energy because that's all you really have in life.

106. Stephen "Wonderboy" Thompson

"No matter how much it hurts, you gotta stay focused on what you're there for and your goals; just don't give up."

If Lyoto Machida did more than anyone to restore the credibility of karate, Stephen Thompson proved that it wasn't a fluke or just the singular talent of one special person.

"Wonderboy"'s unmistakable karate style flummoxed opponents and gave him spectacular wins in the UFC welterweight (170 lbs) division as well. Although he has not quite matched Machida's accomplishments with a UFC championship belt of his own, he is widely regarded as one of the most accomplished strikers in UFC history and scored a draw and a narrow majority decision in his two title shots so far.

What both Machida and "Wonderboy" have in common, apart from their incredible and unique karate skills, is their discipline and focus. The extra emphasis on the mental game and meditation in their traditional martial art background no doubt helped a lot in that area.

Putting in time and discipline to meditation can help just as much in areas outside of martial arts too.

107. Nate Diaz

"I'm trying to stay focused on what I'm doing. I don't want a whole lot of things going on—people to call back, or text messages or whatever. I chill out, relax a little bit, and then I don't have those issues."

Nate Diaz's quote above shows the benefits of simplifying your lifestyle on your overall ability to focus.

It's easy to say that one should focus more on the most important things you can control in your life right now, but it's another to actually do it when surrounded by distractions. The key: cut down on the distractions. You don't have to put effort into ignoring what doesn't exist. You can't always control your own impulses, emotions, and reactions to tempting things, but you can make it a lot easier on yourself by controlling your environment.

Nate Diaz, like his brother Nick, much prefers a simpler life of training.

They both famously dislike media obligations and other distractions meant to help hype up a fight, and that's because they both know they are naturally susceptible to distractions. So are most people if they are honest with themselves. What the Diaz brothers do that's wise is make every effort to cut those distractions out of their life so they can focus on their training and their fight as much as possible.

Their results speak for themselves.

108. Chris Weidman

"One of the big things that I focus on is not having regrets, just taking every opportunity that I have and going for it."

A common theme among many of the quotes of the great champions of MMA, of which Chris Weidman is no exception, is the theme of avoiding regrets by taking opportunities as they come.

As the first man in the UFC to defeat Anderson Silva and take his middleweight (185 lbs) championship belt, Weidman will go down in history as a giant slayer for that alone. The true power of his focus was proven by his ability to come back from a horrific leg break in 2021. Doctors told him he would need at least eight weeks to walk without crutches and six to 12 months before he could resume training, but he was back on his feet doing light training within seven weeks.

What does his quote imply about focus, though? Isn't being open to taking opportunities as they come a contradiction to staying focused on what you're doing? Not if you are focused on the right things. If you are staying focused on accomplishing long-term goals by doing what you need to do in the present, being open to a new opportunity will not contradict any of that as long as it is an opportunity to better accomplish your long-term goals or slightly adjust them to be even more in line with your core values.

Therefore, it's important to understand your core values and carefully craft your goals in accordance with them; that is how you understand and resolve the apparent contradiction between staying dedicated and focused while simultaneously being open to new opportunities.

In this way, you can quickly and efficiently sort out what is a meaningless distraction and what is a valuable opportunity.

109. José Aldo

"Even parrots talk. I don't care about what they say."

José Aldo, the all-time great UFC featherweight (145 lbs) champion and bantamweight (135 lbs) contender, has a great, snappy quote about what not to focus on: the words of your opponents.

As a prizefighter, Aldo knows as well as anyone that trash-talking is part of the game. He famously endured a withering hail of it in the run-up to his match with Conor McGregor. Unfortunately for him, it appeared to have actually had some effect on him, causing him to abandon his usual, more measured style and rush in to exchange punches immediately. McGregor was ready, and scored a very fast and very decisive knockout to end Aldo's legendary 18-fight win streak and take his featherweight belt.

Aldo learned a lot from that match, and we can too. From then on, Aldo dedicated himself to focusing on his own training and performance. Although he is now well into his fighting career, his only defeats since dropping down to bantamweight are an extremely close split decision loss to Marlon Moraes and a defeat to division champion Petr Yan. He racked up two quick wins after that and is on pace to get another shot to fight for UFC gold.

All he has to do is stay focused and ignore the parrots and other similar distractions.

110. Khabib "The Eagle" Nurmagomedov

"I train, eat, sleep, and repeat."

This simple but powerful summary of the life of "The Eagle" explains how Khabib Nurmagomedov was able to maintain championship form so consistently for so long.

Unlike many other champions in MMA, and in other sports too for that matter, Khabib never let success become his greatest enemy. He never got complacent, he never got comfortable, and he never felt entitled to fame, fortune, luxury, or deference beyond simple respect. He simply went on training, eating, and sleeping. That kind of rock-solid focus is what sustained championship runs are truly made of.

What we can learn from Khabib is that if you want to keep getting the same results, you must keep doing the same things that got you those results. If you achieve your goals, don't change yourself. Don't abandon the core values that got you to those goals. Don't be complacent or cocky. Keep up your discipline and your good habits, and you will keep having success.

If you find that too difficult to do, you may want to think about re-examining your core values. If you're sure that you're after what is really valuable to you, then you may also want to consider cutting down on distractions as much as possible.

111. Nick Diaz

"I'm just going to do what I always do: train. And when it's time to fight, I go fight."

Nick Diaz reiterates a common theme of this chapter: focus on what you have to do today and save the worry about what you have to do later for later.

One thing the Diaz brothers have noticed is that the best way to allay worries about the future is to be confident that you're putting in the work necessary today. By staying focused on what you need to do in the present, and finishing what you must finish now, you can stave off a great deal of anxiety about the future.

The purpose of anxiety is to motivate us to prepare for potential difficulties. The problem comes when that anxiety paralyses us or saps our energy and actually gets in the way of our preparation rather than motivating it.

If you find yourself worrying a lot about the future, sometimes one of the best things to try first is to break down your potential future problems into things that can be worked on right now, today, and then focus on those things one at a time.

That's what your anxiety is trying to tell you to do, and once you get to work on it, you may find your anxiety falling away.

112. Joanne Calderwood

"You have to stay focused out there, and you can't get caught up in your emotions."

Joanne Calderwood's quote above touches on one of the toughest aspects of staying focused: the role that emotions play in moments of heightened stress.

It's easy to take an overly simplistic view that emotions are just distractions that have to be ignored so you can focus, but the reality is that human emotions are far more fundamental than that view would imply. Emotions are called emotions because they are what gets our body in motion in the first place; without emotions, you wouldn't do anything at all. The logical result of 'ignoring your emotions' would be just staying still, lying in bed or wherever you are, and not moving anywhere. Obviously, that's not a recipe for success.

The real key is to channel your emotions.

Your emotions will give you energy and strength, and your focus will keep that energy and strength most efficiently channelled on accomplishing your objective. Humans cannot be emotionless robots as our emotions are what make us work, but we can be rational, logical, and focused on how to channel the energy that our emotions give us in order to best accomplish our goals and overcome whatever challenge is in front of us.

Good training will teach you how to do that, even in the heat of the most intense moments.

113. "The Notorious" Conor McGregor

"I wish everyone well, but you need to focus on yourself. You need to stop putting your hand out. Everyone wants hand-outs. Everyone wants things for free. You've got to put in the work. You've got to grind. You've got to go through the struggle, and you've got to get it."

Conor McGregor sometimes has a rather harsh way of putting things, but the core of his advice above is to focus on what you can do for yourself rather than on what others can or should do for you.

For some people, this advice no doubt comes off as needlessly callous or even ignorant, while for others, it rings of nothing but simple common sense. At the end of the day, everyone needs to figure out what they think about it for themselves, and to try to do so with honesty and good faith.

Perhaps the most balanced way to look at it is, if you're unhappy with where you are in life or what you have, ask yourself, "What have I done to deserve better than what I have? What sacrifices have I made in the past to improve my present today? What sacrifices could I make now to improve my future?"

If you can focus on answering those questions, and then doing what the answers imply, you'll put yourself in the best possible position to succeed and get on the road to where you really want to be.

114. Rickson Gracie

"Not the past, not the future. Life is now."

This philosophical and poetic statement by the great Rickson Gracie perfectly sums up the main theme of this chapter.

Life is what is happening to us right now; it's what we experience right now. The past is nothing more to us than our memories of it, and how it created the lives and the world that we're living in right now. The future is nothing more to us than our anticipations and predictions that might or might not ever actually happen. The future means nothing solid until it turns into now, the present, and the life we are actually living.

By definition, only the now actually matters; the past and the future matter only in how they affect what you're feeling and doing right now.

When you understand that, it can help you maximise your ability to focus on what you're doing. Everything that you do now is the result of past forces and will affect your future life, but you can only live now, act now, and change or improve things now. Every moment is precious. It's really all we have.

Life is nothing but a lifetime of moments, and, at the end of your life, all that you will have left to ask yourself is how many of those moments you savoured and how many of them you wasted and let slip away.

Chapter 7:

Humility

Humility, like great art, is tough to define precisely, but everyone knows it when they see it.

So, rather than wasting too many words trying to define precisely what humility is, this chapter will illustrate it through the quotes and experiences of some of the last people in the world you might expect to be experts on humility: 26 of the greatest champions of MMA.

With these quotes and anecdotes, you'll observe many aspects of humility and understand how it's a valuable part of a happy and successful life, whether you're a prizefighter or anything else.

You'll see that being humble isn't just something you should endure for a while or until you 'get good'; it's a lifelong character trait, a core value.

115. José Aldo

"We win, lose, but learn in the defeat."

José Aldo spent most of his career firmly in the winning column.

His 18-fight win streak–especially considering so much of it was as a top contender and then world champion, fighting the toughest men in the world–has gone down in history as one of the all-time great streaks in MMA. Then, add in the fact that his only early loss was when he jumped up to lightweight (155 lbs), and his featherweight (145 lbs) winning streak was actually 25! However, that all came to an end after his crushing 13-second defeat to Conor McGregor.

Most people would have lost more than their belt and their winning streak after such a defeat. Not José Aldo, though. He bounced back and continued to put up incredible performances against the best of the best, earning two more title shots at featherweight and now rapidly climbing the ranks of bantamweight. José Aldo's secret is that he always remained humble.

He was born a humble kid in the streets of Rio De Janeiro, and he never let the fame and money of his championship run go to his head in any of the wrong ways. When his loss did finally come, he did what very few other people would have done in his situation; he simply brushed himself off, chalked it up as just another learning experience, and got right back to the business of fighting and beating the best fighters in the world.

116: Carlos "The Natural Born Killer" Condit

"It's the quiet, humble guy that's not saying anything. That's the really dangerous one."

Carlos Condit could be talking about himself here, or perhaps his greatest rival in the UFC welterweight (170 lbs) division, Georges St. Pierre.

Either way, what he's saying rings true. "The Natural Born Killer" earned his intimidating nickname not for anything he said before or after any of his matches, but for his ruthless efficiency in dispatching opponents with a well-rounded offence that had him looking for the finish every minute of every fight.

His list of victims includes big talkers and big names like Dan Hardy, Nick Diaz, Rory MacDonald, Jake Ellenberger, and Thiago Alves. The list of names of people who survived to defeat Condit in his prime is much shorter: Georges St. Pierre and "Ruthless" Robbie Lawler. Condit gave both some of the toughest fights of their careers, losing only just by very narrow decisions.

Condit's quote articulates something we all intuitively understand: a humble person who says nothing and listens to everything is someone who is both learning a lot and doesn't feel the need to compensate for anything with words.

That's a person who can let their actions and ability do the talking for them.

117. Matt Hughes

"When you lose, say little. When you win, say less."

Matt Hughes is one of the great pioneers of the UFC welterweight (170 lbs) division.

He took the UFC welterweight title in UFC 34 in 2001, in a thrilling match with jiu-jitsu expert Carlos Newton. Newton sunk a very deep triangle choke on Hughes, a wrestling specialist, and in an effort to escape, Hughes picked Newton up over his head. Then, the choke rendered Hughes unconscious, and he went limp— which had the effect of slamming Newton over six feet down onto his own head and knocking him out instantly. The referee, not knowing that Hughes had ever gone out, awarded him the KO victory, and Hughes took home the UFC welterweight championship with one of the all-time great slam KOs.

Hughes dominated the division for years until finally being surpassed by fellow legend Georges St. Pierre, and his penchant for slams made him a star and attracted a ton of fans to the new welterweight division and to lower weight class bouts in general. Through it all, he remained humble.

A perfect example: even though he beat Newton, he freely and openly acknowledged that he himself had been put to sleep by the triangle choke, and he went straight back to camp to work on his submission skills and defence. That work paid off in his first match with GSP: he kept his title for a little longer by submitting Georges St. Pierre with an armbar.

118. Nick Diaz

"I may not be able to keep fighting for money for a living, but I will always have to fight for my dignity because that's who I am."

Nick Diaz has a way with words that don't necessarily scream 'humble', but one thing this quote illustrates is that humility is not in contradiction with dignity.

Being humble doesn't mean you ever have to sacrifice your dignity. In fact, being humble means you will usually never be asked to. It's always the arrogant show-off that people love to see taken down a few pegs.

By staying humble, you will almost never be put in that position, and when you are, generally anyone else who sees it will take your side. If you do find yourself having to fight for your dignity, don't despair. That doesn't make you cocky or arrogant. At worst, it makes you misunderstood.

If you are truly humble, you'll be able to learn from the experience and how to avoid it in the future.

119. Max "Blessed" Holloway

"I am white belt minded. You can always get better. Once you think you're good, you're in for a rude awakening."

Mixed martial arts are one of the best disciplines in the world for keeping you humble.

The reason is right there in the name: it's mixed. Sure, with ten or so years of dedicated training, a talented athlete can master a martial art. But that's just one; in MMA, you can be training with or facing off against masters of any of a dozen or more effective martial arts.

The generally accepted wisdom is that MMA consists of at least three main aspects: stand-up, takedowns and submissions. You need to be able to deal with masters of all three of those to have any chance of climbing the ranks in MMA. The problem being, of course, that that would imply needing at least 30 years of training even for a dedicated and talented athlete. Even if you start at ten years old, that makes you 40 before you've mastered everything. Obviously, that doesn't add up well, considering the average athletic prime is somewhere between 25 and 35 years old.

What it means is that no matter how good you are, you're always going to be training with and fighting against people who are better than you in some aspect. If you aren't humble enough to accept that and learn from every one of those opportunities, you're going to get stuck and hit a wall sooner rather than later.

120. Georges "Rush" St. Pierre

"The truth is that I didn't start as a winner. When I was a kid, I was just another reject. I started at the bottom. I think all winners do."

Georges St. Pierre is another one of those people whose accomplishments are way out of proportion with how humbly he carries himself.

Of course, St. Pierre never comes off as meek or unconfident, but then again, confusing those with humility is a mistake. St. Pierre comes off as is confident in his abilities but also always open and willing to learn more. He's also not entitled or arrogant: he doesn't demand respect or deference, but he is as respectable as he is respectful, and therefore he gets it anyway.

His quote also points out a truth that we all inherently understand: True champions very often start from the bottom. Starting from the bottom teaches you a lot about yourself, and about the value and importance of the effort, it takes to climb.

The expression, "Their confidence outweighs their ability", is very rarely applied to winners or champions. People who have always had life easy, and handed to them on a plate, may not find as much success or do much on their own to improve their position because of complacency and because it's just so hard to be humble if you grew up with everything that other people had to work much harder to get for themselves.

In a way, being born into harder circumstances can be an advantage when it makes you humble enough to be open to seizing opportunities as they come.

121. "Thug" Rose Namajunas

"No one is perfect, but without honesty, you've got nothing."

This is a bit of a cryptic quote to understand, but Rose makes a great point here.

What she's referring to is the old expression that 'perception is reality'. In other words, something doesn't become real to you until you perceive it. This can lead to people being dishonest with themselves in order to blind themselves to their own faults and weaknesses in an effort to keep them from being real. However, that line of thinking actually leads to far more harm.

If you aren't honest with yourself, if you willfully blind *yourself*, you've actually got nothing. By taking away your own ability to perceive reality, you've taken away everything from yourself. If perception is reality, the failure to perceive means there is no reality.

The only solution, as Rose so succinctly implies, is to be humble, to accept that you aren't perfect, as nobody is, and to perceive yourself honestly. Yes, that will reveal your own flaws and weaknesses to you, which is unpleasant. However, that unpleasantness is a necessary part of dealing with your weaknesses, learning from your failures, and growing and getting stronger in the future.

122. Stipe Miocic

"I fell for my own hype. I had too many people saying I couldn't be beat, and I actually fell for it."

Referring to his loss to Francis Ngannou, Stipe Miocic makes a difficult admission with this quote.

Sometimes, when you realise you haven't been humble enough and paid the price for your arrogance, the first step to dealing with it is swallowing that humble pie and admitting it. It's easy to dislike someone who has clearly let their success go to their head, but it's hard not to feel sympathetic towards someone willing to admit it when it happens. Stipe Miocic will go down as one of the all-time great heavyweights in UFC history no matter what happens, but his humility in defeat gives him the best chance of extending his legacy even further.

In the meantime, we can all take a lesson from Stipe's experience and his quote. Much like Israel Adesanya said in another quote featured above, "You're never as bad as they say you are, and you're never as good as they say you are".

No matter what anyone else says about you, you have to stay honest and true with yourself first and foremost.

123. Alexander "The Great" Volkanovski

"I'm always my hardest critic."

Alexander Volkanovski's quote is a common sentiment among the champions and the best of the best in any given field.

If you want to get to the top of any challenging and competitive field, you cannot sit around and wait for others to criticise you and tell you where to improve. Every day that you waste in complacency waiting for something bad to happen or for someone else to notice where you could be doing better is a day that your competition could be using to find and work on their own flaws and weaknesses.

Living in a constant state of self-criticism can be exhausting, no doubt. It's not for everyone. Many people, perhaps most people, are just not cut out to be their own worst critics every minute of every day. It can grind you down.

So, you do have to find your own healthy balance. But if you do want to be the best at something, if you do want to climb to the very top, that's the sacrifice you have to be willing and able to make: to never be satisfied with where you are, and to always be searching out ways to do better.

That's the ultimate form of improvement-oriented humility.

124. Dustin "The Diamond" Poirier

"Everybody has their own path. Everybody peaks at different times."

Dustin Poirier's quote strikes a more optimistic and forgiving tone of humility.

Sometimes, humility means not putting too much pressure on yourself all at once. After all, believing that you are fated for some grand destiny, or that your accomplishments are not commensurate with some immense talent you feel you're supposed to have, is not exactly humble.

Humility is about accepting where you are in the world, accepting that you have flaws and imperfections, and being open to ways to work on and improve upon them. Being disappointed with your own path or where you are on your path reeks of entitlement, not humility.

If you are truly humble, you will accept where you are now and look forward to accomplishing more at some point in the future with some patience and some humility about the amount of work and sacrifice it will take in the meantime to get there.

125. Holly "The Preacher's Daughter" Holm

"I still have a lot to learn, and I still have a lot to prove."

It would be hard to imagine a better avatar of the power of humility and grace in the MMA world than Holly Holm.

Despite her numerous world titles in kickboxing and her UFC championship run, Holly Holm remains as humble as ever in her own pursuit of self-improvement. It was her humility that got her to where she is, and it's her humility that has kept her in title contention even as the field has gotten stuffed with absolutely incredible athletes in their prime like Amanda Nunes and Valentina Shevchenko.

It's apparent from her fights that she is indeed still learning from every victory and defeat. After narrowly losing a decision to "Cyborg" Santos, Holm came back with a more aggressive and assertive performance to defeat Megan Anderson. After getting dropped by an early head kick from Amanda Nunes, Holm cleaned up her defence and cruised to two straight victories against Raquel Pennington and Irene Aldana.

As long as Holm stays healthy and humble in victory and defeat, she does indeed have a lot left in her to prove.

126. Frankie "The Answer" Edgar

"You learn a lot as a coach when you sit back and tell someone what to do, and then you realise, 'Hey, I need to start doing that myself'. I think coaching can improve a fighter's game tremendously."

There are few fighters who have more respect from other fighters than Frankie Edgar.

Everyone he's ever fought has commented on his 'gameness', his ability to keep coming and keep trying for the win no matter how much adversity he's under. It's particularly notable given that he spent half his career fighting at lightweight (155 lbs) even though he's a natural featherweight (145 lbs) and often looked noticeably smaller than almost everyone he fought.

His point about coaching, which applies equally well to teaching or training, is a great flipside to the value of humility. When you step into the role of coach, teacher, or trainer, it can be a very humbling experience because now you have a student relying on you to give them the best possible chance at their own success.

If you take the responsibility seriously and with appropriate humility, you will quickly find ways in which your advice should be applied to yourself as well and improve yourself as much as you improve whoever you're coaching.

127. Rickson Gracie

"If you do not speak up when it matters, when would it matter that you speak? The opposite of courage is conformity. Even a dead fish can go with the flow."

As usual, the words of Rickson Gracie have incredible wisdom and power.

Here he speaks of a very common danger or trap of false humility: cowardice disguising itself as humility. It is not humble to allow yourself to be cowed. It is not humble to be too afraid to stand up for what you believe in. As Rickson's poetic imagery makes clear, nobody would watch a dead fish floating down a river and admire it for its humility.

Humility is being open to others and acknowledging your own flaws and imperfections, but it does not mean you have to forget about your own core values. Humility is accepting defeat with grace and a desire to learn how to improve and avoid future failure, not giving up and resigning yourself to whatever situation you're trying to overcome.

A humble person can speak up, and they are listened to when they do, because they do not speak from arrogance or cockiness, and their silence does not come from cowardice.

128. Stephen "Wonderboy" Thompson

"To be honest with you, getting knocked out isn't that bad. It's not what everyone makes it out to be."

"Wonderboy" is another one of those fighters who is the epitome of how dangerous the humble man can be.

He eschews anything but the utmost expressions of respect for his opposition, and nobody's attempts to trash talk him have ever gotten under his skin. In response to Dana White awarding the honorary "BMF" (Baddest Motherf**ker) belt to Jorge Masvidal, fans have taken to saying that "Wonderboy" should be given the "NMF" (Nicest Motherf**ker) belt.

What his quote above indicates is another one of the advantages of humility.

In truth, the worst part of getting knocked out for most fighters is how humbling it is. To be rendered unconscious is to be rendered totally helpless by another person and put totally at their mercy.

If you're already humble, this isn't as bad as it would be for someone who's arrogant and needs to see themselves as invincible and unbeatable.

129. Tony "El Cucuy" Ferguson

"Everybody has their good days and their bad days; there's always two sides to a story."

A part of being humble is remembering these wise words of "El Cucuy".

There are two sides to every story, and two sides to this quote as well. Whenever you are on top, you have to remember that you were once on the bottom, and one day you'll be on the bottom again–so stay humble.

Likewise, when you're on the bottom, humility will protect you from the worst pain of humiliation, and help you stay open to the lessons you need to learn to get back on top.

By the same token, when looking at other people, remember that they too have their good days and their bad days. Don't arrogantly write someone off just because you happened to catch them on their worst day. Don't write yourself off either in comparison to them just because you happened to catch them on their best day.

130. Donald "Cowboy" Cerrone

"You see all the movies where people say, 'Don't fight out of anger'? They say that for a reason."

"Cowboy" is talking from his own hard, perhaps humbling experience here.

Going into a fight angry is a great way to end up humbled if not humiliated, and not the least because anger can overcome and replace your own humility in the first place. Anger is a great emotion to motivate you to defend yourself when appropriate: it's a sign that your mind is telling you you're being attacked, abused, or taken advantage of.

In that sense, anger should often be carefully considered and heeded. However, going into a prize-fight angry is giving yourself more energy and motivation than you need to be at your best.

Anger is great for getting you ready for a confrontation. It warns you that a confrontation is necessary to protect yourself. But once it's done that, its job is over. Then, it's time for your humility to reassert itself, to make you open to what you need to be open to in order to resolve your confrontation successfully. Or, in the case of a prize-fight, to make you focused on your own technique, on your opponent, and to maximise your efficiency and chances of victory.

131. Alexander "The Mauler" Gustafsson

"My best advice for mental training is simply to create good habits, in order to build a sense of security and calm around you."

This is wonderful general advice from Alexander Gustafsson.

The way it relates to humility is that humility is one of the good habits that will best contribute to a sense of security and calm around you. Humility makes you calm and secure because it doesn't place undue pressure on you.

It doesn't pretend you are perfect or that you or anyone else is supposed to be perfect. It doesn't pretend that any mistakes or flaws you have are fatal. It doesn't deceive you.

Humility keeps you open to what you need to do to improve yourself, and to what you need to accept about yourself while you work on doing so.

Humility is one of the greatest gifts you can give yourself, and one of the best habits you can cultivate to keep yourself calm and secure.

132. Dana White

"We're all entitled to make mistakes. I'm not one of those guys where if you make a mistake, I'm gonna try to tear your life down and burn it to the ground."

Dana White is another person in the MMA world who doesn't exactly come off as humble most of the time, but in truth, it takes both a great deal of forceful assertiveness and brashness and a great deal of humility to simultaneously manage the egos of hundreds of the greatest fighters in the world on one hand, and investors, advertising and television executives, media, politicians, fans, and more on the other.

If Dana White was actually as arrogant as his worst critics might think he is, he'd have crashed and burned decades ago.

What Dana White says in his quote is a great sentiment on the relationship between humility and forgiveness. If you are humble, you are willing to forgive your own mistakes, and the mistakes of others.

That's a wise way to go through life in general, even more so if you need to manage thousands of complex and difficult relationships like White does.

133. Derrick "The Black Beast" Lewis

"I've been through so much stuff that I hope even my enemies wouldn't have to go through."

Considering Lewis is 6'3, always tips the scales at the heavyweight limit of 265 lbs and has 20 knockouts (most in the first round), in his 25 MMA wins, his opponents must be grateful for his obviously kind and humble nature—at least, outside of the Octagon.

Inside the Octagon, he is one of the most fearsome men you could find yourself facing.

Lewis's quote shows something of his humility, and where it's come from. He spent three and a half years in prison for aggravated assault before discovering MMA and finding his true calling in life. It also shows that he's learned the best possible lesson from it.

Any average guy can wish their enemies suffer what they have suffered; Lewis shows far more wisdom in wishing better for his enemies. That isn't just kind; it's wise. Why wish more pain on anyone, even your enemies? Won't your enemies be that much more likely to hate you too if their lives get harder?

The better the world is for anyone, the better it is for everyone.

134. Amanda "Lioness" Nunes

"I respect my opponents. I learned that from life. I used to think I would step in there, throw one punch, and the other girl would go down and not get up again. Every time I thought that, I lost."

Amanda Nunes must have learned this lesson quickly, considering her very first professional fight was a loss.

Since her final defeat to Cat Zingano in UFC 178, she's had an excellent memory, because she's been on a 12-fight undefeated streak since then. Amanda Nunes's quote shows us one of the ways in which humility helps protect us from ourselves.

If you arrogantly believe your opponent, or whatever challenge you face in life, will be easy for you to overcome, the shock when that doesn't happen can make achieving the success you felt you were entitled to that much more difficult.

Humility prepares you to overcome adversity by expecting it and removing any shock that might have impacted you when it happens.

If it turns out you win easily after all, well, so much the better!

135. Jorge "Gamebred" Masvidal

"I got taught respect because if not, somebody's gonna make you respect them."

Jorge Masvidal comes from a hard culture of respect and humility.

He is an experienced and successful veteran, a pioneer whose career in MMA began in 2003 and who has fought for numerous titles and holds some truly impressive accolades, including the fastest KO in UFC history with his five-second starching of the freshly signed ex-Bellator and One FC welterweight (170 lbs) champion Ben Askren in 2019. Although he is quick to anger and willing to use that anger to defend his honour and his dignity, that doesn't make him any less humble or respectful when it counts.

He was not born into an easy life, and he has not had an easy career either. What he has had is decades of struggle to get where he is, and both the humility and the dignity that that entails.

His career has seen some humbling defeats, like the inverted triangle by Toby Imada that was the submission of the year in 2009 and graces highlight reels to this day. However, he has also had some amazing triumphs, like being one of the extremely few fighters to ever stop Nate Diaz in one of the fights of the year for 2019.

You cannot have great triumphs like that without learning from the humbling defeats first.

136. Michael "The Count" Bisping

"The underdog status suits me just fine."

Michael Bisping's bold personality and quick wit probably don't always come off as humble to most fans–especially American fans during his days of rivalry with American stars like Matt Hamill, Luke Rockhold and Dan Henderson–but the fact that Bisping has always been so comfortable as an underdog shows his genuine humility.

Bisping has always known that MMA stardom was going to be an uphill battle for a British kickboxer in an age where the sport was dominated by American wrestlers and Brazilian BJJ and Muay Thai experts.

Bisping's humility gave him the willingness to learn from and adapt to those disciplines, ultimately incorporating them into his game and figuring out how to counter them. It took him over a decade of struggling as an underdog, but he got his championship belt in the end.

That's the true power of humility.

137. "Iron" Michael Chandler

"Integrity eclipses image."

How humble can a man who took on Mike Tyson's nickname really be?

Well, Chandler didn't do it out of arrogance: he was given that nickname by his team after meeting and getting advice on humility from "Iron" Mike Tyson himself. Tyson warned Chandler: "Champ, it's easy coming up. Then as soon as you get the belt and everyone's gunning for you, every single person's looking at you, they're waking up, thinking about fighting you, they're going to bed, thinking about fighting you."

Chandler took that advice to heart, and in the quote above, has some wise words of his own. To 'eclipse' is to cover over, to block from sight; the 'image' is what we want to show the world, but sooner or later, it is always eclipsed by our 'integrity', what is really there.

If you are humble, honest, and you have integrity, that will eclipse any image.

138. Robert "Bobby Knuckles" Whittaker

"Who am I to tell people what to do with their own careers and how they're doing?"

Robert Whittaker shows some of the wisdom of humility with this quote, in response to requests to comment on other fighters.

Some fighters would seize the chance to call someone out, try to generate a little excitement for a match, try to get some social media mentions going and boost their own stock. Robert Whittaker recognises that game for the trap that it is, though. If you have talent, you can let it speak for itself. If you have dignity and humility, you will.

"Bobby Knuckles" has always let his hands speak for him in the Octagon.

That's why he has a huge and dedicated fan base, and that's why he's put himself into championship contention multiple times.

139. Gina Carano

"It's a very big deal to me to remain the same person because I know all of this is going to be gone one day, and I'm just going to have myself."

Gina Carano was one of the first and brightest stars of women's MMA, a true pioneer, and she seemed to have a unique ability to appreciate that in real-time.

Most stars get swept up in their stardom and quickly lose track of the person they were before they were famous. Most pioneers barely understand what's happening while their sport is blowing up around them.

Gina Carano is the unusual person who managed to avoid both pitfalls and wisely thread the needle of being able to appreciate her stardom without letting it go to her head and change her.

Her humility in the face of her newfound fame and money was what enabled her to do so.

140. Brian "T-City" Ortega

"Sometimes, the best response is no response."

In a world of endless social media sniping and bickering that can seem impossible to escape whether you're an MMA star, a celebrity, a political figure, or just a regular person doing regular stuff, Ortega's quote shows how just a little more humility can be the answer we were looking for all along.

Having the humility to accept a loss gracefully, to grant a point to someone on the other side of some issue, or even just to let bygones be bygones, and to respond simply by not responding, can be the best way out of a difficult situation we really have nothing to gain from.

It can be hard to let some things go, but ultimately what can help us do so is embracing a little bit more humility. If you find yourself angrily preparing a response to something or someone that annoyed you, just ask yourself, in all humility, isn't there something more valuable you could be doing instead?

Chapter 8:

Community

John Donne famously wrote that "No man is an island", and that poem rings as true today as ever.

It is no different in MMA.

Every fighter enters the ring, cage, or Octagon to fight alone. However, every one of them got there with the support of their family and their team, and part of the consequences of the outcome of their match will fall on their family and their team as well, win or lose.

As we've discussed, humans are fundamentally social creatures: our success requires the support and cooperation of others, and their success relies on us as well. We are not in this life alone, and as long as we live, we never will be. As much as our own minds and bodies, our community can help determine our chances of success and happiness.

Our success is in no small part determined by how well we accept and navigate this reality.

Exceptional teams are often behind the greatest MMA fighters (made up of outstanding training partners, coaches, and other support staff). The greatest MMA fighters are also cognisant that they are not just fighting for themselves, but for their team and their family.

They are aware, explicitly and implicitly, that to be on the best teams, they must be the best teammate.

To have brilliant training partners, they have to be brilliant training partners.

To get the best coaches, they must be dedicated and committed students.

To have loving and loyal support around them in life, they also have to be a loving and loyal support for others.

Those who understand and follow this principle—the principle of community explored in this chapter—give themselves the best chances of achieving success in life.

141. Khabib "The Eagle" Nurmagomedov

"When difficult decisions appear in my life, and there are difficult questions to answer…I consult loved ones."

Few people on Earth have more credibility than Khabib Nurmagomedov on the topic of seeking advice from loved ones on difficult decisions.

He was on a 29-fight winning streak, UFC lightweight (155 lbs) champion, at the height of his power and in the prime of his life, when he stepped away from the sport and retired undefeated. Why did he do it? Why did he leave millions of dollars on the table and every possibility of establishing an ironclad legacy of continual dominance that might never be matched?

The answer appears to be quite simply because his mother asked him to.

Khabib's father tragically passed away the year before Khabib officially retired. He finished his last fight, against Justin Gaethje, and promised his mother he would not fight again without his father. No amount of cajoling from the infamously assertive and persuasive Dana White or begging from the fans could change his mind. Khabib's first commitment was to his family, and he proved it once and for all.

What can we learn from this?

Even for the greatest champion, and Khabib is undoubtedly in that conversation, there are things more important than winning more fights and keeping that belt longer. It's surely inspiring to know that Khabib put his promise to his mother over continuing his incredibly successful and lucrative career.

Most of us will never enjoy the kind of success in our fields as Khabib has in his, but most of us can make and keep promises to those we love most in life. If that is more important to Khabib than several more years of dominance and respect at the top of his sport, and the millions of dollars they would bring in, then it should be good enough for all of us.

142. Cain Velasquez

"You need good training partners—because you're only as good as your training partners—and a strong desire to always get better."

Cain Velasquez is one of the greatest heavyweights in UFC history.

His career was unfortunately derailed by a series of injuries, leaving many to wonder 'what if?', but what he did accomplish in his truncated career was spectacular dominance of the UFC heavyweight division in its prime, including two UFC heavyweight (265 lbs) championships. A big part of Cain's success was his excellent team of coaches and training partners at the American Kickboxing Academy.

Velasquez has always understood the importance of the team around you. For anyone who doubts it, look at the accomplishments of AKA (the American Kickboxing Academy): Apart from Cain Velasquez's two heavyweight championships, there is Daniel Cormier's multiple heavyweight and light heavyweight (205 lbs) championships, Khabib Nurmagomedov's all-time great run at lightweight (155 lbs), Luck Rockhold's middleweight (185 lbs) championships, BJ Penn's lightweight (155 lbs) and welterweight (170 lbs) championships, and many more.

It isn't a coincidence that so many of Cain Velasquez's teammates have won the highest honours in MMA;

success breeds success. If you have great partners pushing you and a strong desire to keep up with them, you'll find success together.

143. Dana White

"I'm a loyal person, man, and people who have been good to me in my life, I don't forget, and I stand by them."

UFC President Dana White understands the power of loyalty.

Loyalty can be a tricky thing, though. The cynic might say that loyalty is just a word used to get people to do things in someone else's best interest, not their own. The idealist might say that loyalty is a virtue and virtue is its own reward.

Economists set out to objectively settle the debate and study the concept of loyalty, among other things, in a field of economics called 'game theory'. Specifically, studies done around the thought experiment known as the 'prisoner's dilemma' have shed a lot of light on the actual practical utility of loyalty and disloyalty.

To make a long story short, careful experimentation over the years has proven the value of a strategy called 'optimistic reciprocity'. In this strategy, the best way to act towards others is to begin by trusting them and being loyal to them yourself, and then, in the future, to treat them as they treat you. In the short run, it's possible that your optimism could get taken advantage of. In the long run, however, you can choose not to deal with people who take advantage of you and deal only with those who treat you as well as you treat them.

The liars and cheats that take advantage of others will soon find themselves without anyone willing to deal with them, while those who choose optimistic reciprocity will always have people who are eager to deal with them, while at the same time maintaining the ability to protect themselves over the long run by cutting out anyone who takes advantage of them.

Dana White may or may not be aware of the results of these 'prisoner's dilemma' experiments, but his quote suggests that he understands it perfectly in any case.

144. Charles "Do Bronx" Oliveira

"Why 'Do Bronx'? Because I'm from the slums, those are my roots."

Charles Oliveira is a man who has not lost sight of where he came from and the community that supported him and built him up as a child. As a result of his phenomenal successes in the Octagon, he's in a position where he can give back to the community that raised him and is something that he most certainly does.

The nickname 'Do Bronx' comes from the Bronx borough of New York City and means "from the Bronx". "Bronx" is a slang term used for favelas and poor neighbourhoods.

In one interview, Charles stated, "Bronx is because it's a favela, right? Outskirts, where I come from. Bronx practically came when I went to fight in a [amateur] tournament. [...] And they told me to get them a nickname, I was just Charles Oliveira. When we went to fight some jiu-jitsu championships, they always said 'look at the guys from Bronx, from the favela'. So, I put "Do Bronx" in".

He holds multiple UFC records, including the most submission wins in the organisation's history at 14 and most finishes at 17. At the time of writing, he is number 8 in the UFC men's pound-for-pound rankings and the world champion of the men's 155 lb division, an achievement that he's been working towards for most of his life.

Born to a low-income family in a favela in the tourist town Guarujá, São Paulo, Brazil, Charles had a dream to become a professional football player, like many young boys. At the age of 7, he was diagnosed with a heart murmur and rheumatic fever, and his family were told that he could develop paraplegia.

Despite these challenges, "Do Bronx" was introduced to Brazilian jiu-jitsu by a neighbour. The school's coach offered classes for free to families of low income as part of a social program, and his family also supported the funding of his training by selling snacks and cardboard they found on the streets.

Shortly after one of his most significant career victories over Tony Ferguson, Oliveira donated thousands of dollars worth of food to his home, Guarujá. The town was hit hard by the COVID-19 pandemic and desperately needed help and support.

Oliveira also has a project which sponsors kids to get them off the streets and into a gym, much like the opportunity he was given as a child. It's a beautiful example of how the cycle of community and support comes around to benefit each party over time and of a man who gives back to his community and the people who helped him achieve his dreams.

145. Amanda "Lioness" Nunes

"When people find out how strong and powerful love is, then this world will be a better place. I want to see this happen one day."

This quote might seem a little ironic, coming from someone as fearsome as Amanda Nunes, undoubtedly one of the most intimidating women ever to enter the Octagon.

That only gives it a lot more credibility, though. Nunes also has a particularly unique connection to love and to fighting. She met her wife, UFC strawweight (115 lbs) competitor Nina Nunes (née Ansaroff), through the UFC, and credits her success in the UFC to their relationship. Drawing strength from love isn't just a beautiful story; it's something that really happens every day.

Parents draw the strength to provide from their love of their children; children draw strength to succeed from the love of their parents; husbands and wives draw strength from each other, and soldiers on the battlefield have the courage to fight for their comrades.

The good news is that while you won't see the world be a better place in *one* day, you can see it becoming a better place every day, if you really care and know where to look. Economists and philosophers like Stephen Pinker and Matt Ridley make an excellent case for all the many ways in which the world has gotten so much better over the last few hundred years, and especially over the last couple of generations.

Perhaps more people are discovering the power of love than one might think if you only look at the bad news.

146. Jorge "Gamebred" Masvidal

"I'm not the kind of dude who kicks somebody when they're down."

One could be forgiven for being surprised that this is a Jorge Masvidal quote.

He's been a part of many highlight reels, both the fastest KO in UFC history, and the victim of the submission of the year in Bellator, but what Masvidal is probably even more famous for is his fiery temper and hold-nothing-back attitude in and out of the Octagon.

After a post-fight altercation with Leon Edwards, Masvidal's fame took an enormous jump when he nonchalantly referred to the punches he threw at Edwards backstage as "the three-piece with a soda". The incident and the quote overshadowed what was, in fact, an incredible comeback win against rising star and favourite Darren Till.

Masvidal went on to be awarded the honorary 'BMF' (Baddest Mother F**ker) belt by Dana White for his victory over Nate Diaz, a fighter with a similar attitude in and out of the ring.

All of that stands in contrast to the quote he gives above.

What it shows is not just that people can be complicated and contradictory; it also shows that even someone who will fight anyone to defend what they see as their honour at the drop of a hat still shouldn't want to exploit someone at their lowest. Such a person could never be trusted or respected in the larger community, nor could they respect themselves.

In a roundabout way, Masvidal's quote really is talking about the importance of respect in a community, as well as for oneself.

147. Joanne Calderwood

"You are what you teach, and you teach what you are."

In a phrase that would have sounded very strange just a generation ago, Scottish Muay Thai champion Joanne Calderwood was one of the inaugural stars of the UFC women's strawweight (115 lbs) division.

She competed in season 20 of The Ultimate Fighter to crown the first UFC strawweight champion and came up just short against Rose Namajunas in a performance that earned both fighters the Fight of the Season bonus. Since then, she has remained a top 10 fighter, always in contention for the belt.

Her quote is a beautiful little piece of wisdom about what teaching really means.

When we set out to teach someone else, what we're really trying to do is give them a valuable part of ourselves. You cannot do that if it isn't already a part of you. Likewise, even when you are not consciously setting out to teach, you may often do so anyway by your example. You are always teaching other people who you are by what you do, and other people are always watching and learning. This is an inevitable part of social life and community.

The lesson is to try to always be at your best because that's what you want others to learn from you, and about you.

148. Quinton "Rampage" Jackson

"When the going gets tough, the leeches are nowhere to be found, but the real people—the real friends—are with you through thick and thin.

"Rampage" is another one of those great stars of MMA whose nickname is a lot more famous than his real name.

He was one of the pioneers of the sport and really made his name in Pride FC, considered for a time to be the premier MMA organisation in the world before the UFC eclipsed it in the wake of the success of The Ultimate Fighter. Jackson's career trajectory has given him the personal perspective to talk about leeches and true friends.

He began as a popular underdog: he was matched against dominant veterans like the legendary Kazushi Sakuraba, Igor Vovchanchyn, Chuck Liddell and Wanderlei Silva right from the beginning of his career, but his unique combination of boxing skills, wrestling slams, and big personality on the microphone made him an immediate fan favourite, win, or lose.

As "Rampage" gained the experience to match his natural talents, his career finally peaked in the UFC, where he defeated Chuck Liddell a second time and claimed the UFC light heavyweight (205 lbs) championship. After the UFC bought out Pride FC, a 'title unification match' with the Pride middleweight (205 lbs) champion, Dan Henderson, was scheduled. "Rampage" won that bout too and became the undisputed best 205 lb fighter in the world. However, after he later lost his belt by a judges' decision to Forrest Griffin, injuries and personal problems hampered "Rampage's" quest to regain his peak.

Quinton Jackson has been at the very summit of MMA achievement and ventured through many of its valleys. His experiences have taught him the value of having real friends who will always stand by you.

149. "Thug" Rose Namajunas

"I learned that love is a much more sustainable energy to draw on than hate."

Rose Namajunas shares a wise and beautiful insight with this quote.

When you think about it, it makes perfect sense too. Hate is a powerful emotion, but its use is to motivate us to protect ourselves from some outside threat. It's only as sustainable as our fear of that threat.

If it's a real threat, we tend to prioritise dealing with it until it's gone. If it's more of a vague, ephemeral, intangible threat, we tend to generally just adapt to it and get used to it. Either way, the hate fades.

What lasts a lifetime is our love, for our family and for our dreams. Learning to embrace that love, and to draw on it for your energy, is truly a much healthier and more sustainable way to go through life. If you are relying on hate for your energy, you'll constantly find yourself having to make more enemies to sustain, and that's a challenging way to go through life.

It's better by far to learn to let go of hate and get your energy from your love and the love of those who love you back.

150. Dustin "The Diamond" Poirier

"I don't talk bad about people who I roll with."

This is excellent advice for anyone training in martial arts, and very applicable in numerous other ways.

When you are rolling, or sparring in a stand-up martial art, you are putting a lot of trust in your partner–and they in you–to make the experience mutually productive. It's essential that you both leave your egos at the door when rolling; if someone starts trying to 'win' in order to satisfy their ego, rolling can very quickly turn into fighting, and then not only could someone get hurt, but both sides also lose out on the training and practice benefits of good rolling.

Rolling is meant to be an opportunity to try things out, to see what works and what doesn't, and to improve fundamental technique by leaving strength and muscle out of the equation as much as possible.

As soon as one fighter starts talking bad about another that they roll or spar with, it becomes impossible to leave ego off the mat. Once you've trash-talked a sparring or rolling partner, you've lost them as a partner, and now you have an opponent or someone who just won't interact with you at all. There are plenty of analogues to this in other sports and occupations.

In fact, another meaning of 'to roll with' someone is simply to hang out and spend quality time with them, and Poirier probably intended that double entendre. When you need to put your trust in someone else and have them put their trust in you to succeed mutually, never put that trust at risk by talking about them out of turn. If you have any problems with them, always resolve those problems directly without ever letting anyone else know.

Conclusion

The careers of the greatest champions of MMA were built not just on their raw physical talent, but on their character and wisdom.

The wisdom of fighters is the wisdom of life: It is the wisdom of inspirational figures, many of whom came from nothing, risked everything, sacrificed much, suffered immensely, and prevailed over the greatest of odds.

The self-belief, commitment, courage, positive thinking, mindset, focus, humility, and community of these champions made them who they are and are captured by their own words and stories.

It is up to us, now, to learn from their examples and apply the lessons of their wisdom to our own lives and struggles. That is the great human journey–the journey that has taken us out of caves and into the stars–the journey that brought us together, from warring tribes into a global economic and social community. We have done all this as a species by listening to each other and learning from each other; by keeping a record of our past successes and building upon them with ever higher and more extraordinary achievements.

These champions have built and are building their own legacies of success–now it's your turn to go out and get started on building yours.

Thank you for reading this book.

If you enjoyed it, please leave a review on Amazon. Reviews are the lifeblood of any published work and are crucial in helping others find an audience and share our message with the world. If there is enough interest, stay tuned for volume 2.

Until then, I wish you all the success, health, and happiness in the world.

About the Author

Neil C is the author of The Wisdom of Fighters. He's a life-long student of psychology and philosophy and has been a combat sports fan for over 30 years. As an enthusiastic martial artist, he's trained in Krav Maga, Boxing, Judo, and Kickboxing. He's been punched in the face both literally and metaphorically more times than he dares count! He lives in the UK, and this is his first book.

References

All fighters' professional records and basic biographical information were referenced from UFC.com, Wikipedia.org and Sherdog.com. Additional references are included below.

Ackerman, C. E. (2017, February 28). *What is gratitude and why is it so important? [2019 update]*. PositivePsychology.com. **https://positivepsychology.com/gratitude-appreciation/**

Asrani, A. (2020, October 12) 5 Things You Didn't Know About Charles Oliveira.

Essentially Sports. **https://www.essentiallysports.com/mma-ufc-news-5-things-you-didnt-know-about-charles-oliveira/**

Betway Insider (2021, June 23) Who is Charles Do Bronx? Discover the history of the Brazilian fighter. **https://blog.betway.com/pt/outros-esportes/quem-%C3%A9-charles-do-bronx-**

conhe%C3%A7a-a-hist%C3%B3ria-do-lutador-brasileiro/

Bloom, P. (2021). *The sweet spot : the pleasures of suffering and the search for meaning.* Ecco, An Imprint Of Harpercollinspublishers.

Bull, A. (2009, November 11). *The forgotten story of...Muhammad Ali v Antonio Inoki | Andy Bull.* The Guardian. **https://www.theguardian.com/sport/blog/200 9/nov/11/the-forgotten-story-of-ali-inoki**

Cherry, K. (2019). *Why Cultivating a Growth Mindset Can Boost Your Success.* Verywell Mind. **https://www.verywellmind.com/what-is-a-mindset-2795025**

Christine, M. (2014, August 31). *Claudinha Gadelha se divide entre as lutas do UFC e os estudos para ser delegada.* Extra Online. **https://extra.globo.com/esporte/lutas/claudin ha-gadelha-se-divide-entre-as-lutas-do-ufc-os-estudos-para-ser-delegada-13774268.html**

Crenshaw, D. (2021). *Myth of Multitasking: How Doing It All Gets Nothing Done (2nd Edition) (Time Management Skills).* Mango Media.

Crouch, J. (2018, October 1). *Safety Check | Target Fixation*. United States Parachute Association. **https://uspa.org/p/Article/safety-check-target-fixation#:~:text=Wikipedia%20defines%20target%20fixation%20as**

Downes Jr, W. (2017, March 23). *UFC superstar Claudia Gadelha is a real-life superhero armed with a law degree for fighting crime in Brazil.* The Sun. **https://www.thesun.co.uk/sport/3158803/ufc-womens-superstar-claudia-gadelha-is-real-life-super-hero-with-plans-for-fighting-crime-in-brazils-special-forces-armed-with-law-degree-studied-for-around-mma-training/**

Fontane Pennock, S. (2016, September 5). *The Hedonic Treadmill - Are We Forever Chasing Rainbows?* PositivePsychology.com. **https://positivepsychology.com/hedonic-treadmill/**

Garbrandt, C., & Dagostino, M. (2018). *The pact: a UFC champion, a boy with cancer, and their promise to win the ultimate battle.* W Publishing Group, An Imprint Of Thomas Nelson.

Harris, S. (2018). *Waking Up.* Waking Up. **https://wakingup.com/**

Hunt, M., & Mckelvey, B. (2017). *Born to fight*. Sphere.

Iole, K. (2017, January 27). *Once homeless on the streets of Paris, Francis Ngannou on the verge of making his dream come true.* Sports.yahoo.com. https://sports.yahoo.com/news/once-homeless-on-the-streets-of-paris-francis-ngannou-on-the-verge-of-making-his-dream-come-true-195847882.html

Johnson, D. (n.d.). *MightyGaming - Twitch.* Www.twitch.tv. https://www.twitch.tv/mightygaming

Kuhn, S. (2019). *Prisoner's Dilemma (Stanford Encyclopedia of Philosophy).* Stanford.edu. https://plato.stanford.edu/entries/prisoner-dilemma/

Lynch, J., Prihodova, L., Dunne, P. J., Carroll, A., Walsh, C., McMahon, G., & White, B. (2018). Mantra meditation for mental health in the general population: A systematic review. *European Journal of Integrative Medicine, 23*(23), 101–108. https://doi.org/10.1016/j.eujim.2018.09.010

Mills, K., & Vyse, S. (2021). *Speaking of Psychology: The psychology of superstition, with Stuart Vyse, PhD.* Apa.org. https://www.apa.org/research/action/speaking-of-psychology/superstition

Nag, S. (2021, June 9). *Nate Diaz reveals why he does triathlons in between fights*. Www.sportskeeda.com. **https://www.sportskeeda.com/mma/news-it-gets-sh-t-together-nate-diaz-points-similarities-triathlons-mma**

Nahta, S. (2021, May 10). *How Did Michael Chandler Earn the Nickname "Iron"*. Sportsmanor. **https://www.sportsmanor.com/how-did-michael-chandler-earn-the-nickname-iron/**

"No Man is an Island" - John Donne. (2019). Cs.dal.ca. **https://web.cs.dal.ca/~johnston/poetry/island .html**

Osborne, C., & BBC Sport. (2014, November 4). "I'm not a thug or a cage fighter". *BBC Sport*. **https://www.bbc.com/sport/29879419**

Pinker, S., Ridley, M., De Botton, A., Gladwell, M., & Griffiths, R. (2016). *Do humankind's best days lie ahead? : Pinker and Ridley vs. De Botton and Gladwell*. House Of Anansi Press Inc.

Renault, M. (1976). *The nature of Alexander*. Pantheon Books.

Reuters. (2021, April 20). UFC-owner Endeavor aims for over $10 bln valuation in second IPO attempt. *Reuters*.

https://www.reuters.com/business/media-
telecom/ufc-owner-endeavor-aims-over-16-bln-
valuation-second-ipo-attempt-2021-04-20/

Russell, W. (2020, February 5). *Jung — How to Integrate your Shadow.* Medium. https://medium.com/@willrussell_46069/jung
-how-to-integrate-your-shadow-72e6b135461c

Scott Barry Kaufman. (2019, June 7). *In-Group Favoritism Is Difficult to Change, Even When the Social Groups Are Meaningless.* Scientific American Blog Network. https://blogs.scientificamerican.com/beautiful
-minds/in-group-favoritism-is-difficult-to-
change-even-when-the-social-groups-are-
meaningless/

Sherdog.com, & Probst, J. (2010, January 19). *Sherdog's 2009 Awards: The Complete List - Knockout of the Year.* Sherdog. https://www.sherdog.com/news/articles/3/Sh
erdogs-2009-Awards-The-Complete-List-22133

Smith, J. P. (2012, March 6). *Roots of Fight: Helio Gracie vs. Masahiko Kimura.* Bleacher Report. https://bleacherreport.com/articles/1092770-
roots-of-fight-helio-gracie-vs-masahiko-kimura

Tarantola, A. (2021, May 3). *How social media recommendation algorithms help spread hate.* Engadget. **https://www.engadget.com/how-social-media-recommendation-algorithms-help-spread-online-hate-180032029.html**

Vaish, A., Grossmann, T., & Woodward, A. (2008). Not all emotions are created equal: The negativity bias in social-emotional development. *Psychological Bulletin,* *134*(3), 383–403. **https://doi.org/10.1037/0033-2909.134.3.383**

Printed in Great Britain
by Amazon

85277829R00169